T0068844

On Life, Death, and This and That of the Rest

THE SWISS LIST

On Life, Death, and This and That of the Rest

THE FRANKFURT LECTURES ON POETICS

URS WIDMER

Translated by Donal McLaughlin

LONDON NEW YORK CALCUTTA

swiss arts council
prɔhelvetiɔ

This publication has been supported by a grant
from Pro Helvetia, Swiss Arts Council

Seagull Books, 2017

First published in 2007 as *Vom Leben, vom Tod und vom Übrigen auch dies und
das* by Urs Widmer © Diogenes Verlag, Zurich

English translation © Donal Mclaughlin, 2012

First published in English translation by Seagull Books, 2013

A first draft of this translation was produced
during a residency at Translation House Looren, near Zurich.

ISBN   978 0 8574 2 528 7

British Library Cataloguing-in-Publication Data
A catalogue record for this book is available from the British Library

Typeset in Cochin by Seagull Books, Calcutta, India
Printed and bound by Maple Press, York, Pennsylvania, USA

CONTENTS

On Deviating from the Norm

Ladies and Gentlemen,

I am pleased to be invited to the university here in Frankfurt and to be asked to give the Lectures on Poetics this semester. I intend to give a lecture that is largely free of anecdote, one in which I don't refer to my own books and plays but speak instead about other people's creations. I am probably the type of person who is more likely to confess something when discussing a third party. — At the outset, however, I do have to tell you how many, for me, crucial things connect me, and how much, with Frankfurt and the people who once lived here, or still do. When well over forty years ago, I first visited Frankfurt, I was nominally of age, it's true, and even possessed a driving licence, but otherwise, I looked like an overgrown boy who had been forced by some uneasy fate to wear long trousers and a smart jacket. Back then, you see, one armed oneself with a tie and a smart jacket if one dared to venture abroad, and here at the uni, students addressed one another formally.

It was my driving skills that moved my father to do something most uncharacteristic—he was a home bird really, not someone to leave the nest—and inform me, from one moment to the next, that we were going to Frankfurt, right away, as Klaus Nonnenmann—we were friends of his, and he, in turn, was on first-name terms with the rest of the literary world—was throwing a party, the mother of all parties, and he had to go, my father reckoned, and so had I, and our car. (My father, an old-school intellectual, of course couldn't drive.)—And so we set off. Our car was a first-generation 2CV—the window wipers only wiped if you were racing along; in town traffic, they squeaked back and forth, merely, as if fatally ill; and if the car was at a standstill, they didn't move at all, rainy squall or not.— We raced along the motorway—with the window wipers working—at an average of a good sixty kmph, my contented father beside me with his gift of a huge lump of air-dried meat on his knee—a Grisons speciality. I experienced real traffic for the first time—traffic didn't yet exist in Switzerland; any more than three or four cars between you and the horizon was unthinkable—and died a thousand deaths. In Frankfurt, at Nonnenmann's place, an attic flat near the Eschenheim Tower, the party of all parties was indeed happening, and I met, at a single stroke, all the big names in German literature at the time.— Nonnenmann, let me tell you, was a wonderful author, who had only a quarter of one lung (the other three-quarters having gone to pot in the War) and smoked two packs of

Rothändle a day. He was the author of a novel more or less forgotten now, *Teddy Flesh oder Die Belagerung von Sagunt*, that will one day secure him a place on the Olympus of literature, which had just appeared at the time. I don't think that was the reason for the party. Promotion, as we know it now, wasn't done back then. — It was a splendid party — wine, women, song. I learnt that evening that German literature was also capable of that. — The next day, my father and I took the huge lump of air-dried meat home again. Apart from Max Frisch, no one had eaten any because the Germans then — like Swiss farmers even now — didn't eat anything they didn't know.

By the time I moved over here not too many years later, I had become a tad more adult. I now drove an R4, and I had a wife. Siegfried Unseld employed me at his wonderful publishing house as an editor for contemporary German literature and casually whispered at the interview, that well, you know, he was no spring chicken any more, and that this beautiful publishing house would one day need a successor, yes, indeed, and I should always bear that in mind when working flat out for 1,200 marks, net. — I nodded, worked flat out but, somehow or other, wasn't to become his successor. — I remained in Frankfurt for seventeen years, seventeen rich and fruitful years, and wrote — if I am counting right — ten books of prose and six plays. I experienced 1968, that wild period, here; years in which the property speculators' wrecking balls raged through Westend so powerfully that, if I had been away for a week or two, I could barely find my way home when I got back, and was glad my house, at least, was still standing. — Here at the uni, I also listened to one or two of my predecessors giving these lectures, without the thought ever entering my mind that, one day, I might follow them. — Back then, only very big shots were invited. Either I've also become a big shot or nowadays lesser species also get a chance to tuck in — after the lions, elephants and crocodiles, it's the turn of the hares and the church mice among us. — At the end of 1984, we — my wife, my child and I — returned to Switzerland. Something I did with curiously mixed feelings. On the one hand, in those seventeen years, I had become something of a local, much more a *German* writer than one from Helvetia. On the other hand, over the years, the differences had become clearer and clearer to me. To begin with, I'd thought, my God, what is the difference supposed to be between someone from Basel and someone from Frankfurt? Same language, same culture. — The difference lay, of course, in the different histories. I learnt that it does indeed make a difference whether one truly, really has to live and suffer fascism on a daily basis, and the war soon after, or whether, like my parents and I, one sees it through the perimeter fence and fears for one's life, but is not at its mercy, or only in the form of those trace elements that the wind of the zeitgeist also blew into Switzerland.

I'd written a doctoral thesis on this topic too! About the years of fascism having, in addition to everything else, devastated the German language. German, once so beautifully soft, had in those twelve murderous years become a one-dimensional linguistic dummy, a language reduced to hollow phrases, with almost every word infected by the lies, the false realities of the dictatorship. Every sensitive human being felt that but it was the writers, the poets, who suffered the most from the depravity of the language; the young writers most of all, as they had no memory of a before and felt they had the energy to begin again, from scratch, to create a different future. They sensed how much their language had rotted, but knew no other.

The generation of those who began to write after 1945 was thus in a place where German literature had never ever been before. They didn't have at their disposal, as all the generations before them, a secure fund of language and thought. A taken-for-granted norm that, as for every new generation, could — or necessarily *would* — lead to friction between them and itself as a result of their deviations from it, in the form of new and different contexts, boldness or impudence, all of which, however, were building, as always in the past, on the firm foundations of a stable tradition. (Of course, the First World War had already left the world of the time in pieces. Perhaps we should add the damage after 1914 to that which followed 1933.) The young post-1945 writers, in any case, no longer had *any* language. Every word proved to be — let's say — sick, and they had at their disposal no — let's say — healthy words, arrived at on their own merits. ('Healthy' itself was one of the sickest words, for what was termed 'healthy' under fascism —

healthy popular sentiment, healthy humour, healthy thinking—was simply a callous readiness to inflict violence and commit murder.) It was a desperate situation and many did despair. All the same, it was the young writers who at least recognized the hopelessness of the situation. To quote Herbert Achternbusch's bon mot, they didn't have a chance but they took it. They were, to use Wolfgang Borchert's term, a 'lost generation', and that was, indeed, more than mere pathos and rhetoric. That was the reality. Ilse Aichinger, in her first novel, *Herod's Children*, published in 1948, and almost the only significant prose work of those early years of a new beginning, has the children attempt on their own initiative, as if it were on the curriculum in their school of life, to unlearn the German language. But that too proves impossible. 'It's the twelfth hour now,' one child sighs. 'And we haven't managed to unlearn a single word.'[1]—This consciousness led to concepts such as *Kahlschlag* ('clearing')—Wolfgang Weyrauch coined the term—and *Stunde Null* ('hour zero'). But, of course, time couldn't be stopped back then either and like before it continued to carry old scrap forward relentlessly.

Back then, by the way, I read *all* the authors who published their first book between 1945 and 1948. I may well have overlooked one or two, but it was a very doable task. It wasn't as if there were many. But only a few tried to work their way towards that deviation from the general linguistic norm that could have become the seed of that promised new language. Only the most aware of them tried radically to alter the meaning of loaded terms because they couldn't do without them completely. And so they now fought *fanatically* for democracy and no longer, as others had done very recently, for the ultimate victory. Only a few really hit out at language itself—Wolfgang Borchert, who died soon after, or Wolfdietrich Schnurre who has been rather unfairly forgotten. Heinrich Böll once described to me, very touchingly, very vividly and very helplessly, how very difficult and loaded the writing of every single sentence was in the first years after the War. Nowadays, it's barely possible to comprehend that it did indeed take the work of about two generations to give back to the German language that minimum of naive potential needed by writers. (We all, of course, need it.) That pinch of innocence, without which writing isn't possible. All those who say, nowadays, that all the books of the post-War years had a weak chest are right, and yet, they should also recall that not a single pilot in the world can fly loops if his plane is on the ground and wingless. German literature, too, has its history of reconstruction. It was difficult work—like that of the ruins generation, dragging stones round. Of course, those who began to reach adulthood around 1933 suffered the most. Even Böll, who went on to secure a Nobel Prize, was always aware he could never quite compensate for this handicap. Aware that when finally, he could look up into the blue sky and breathe fresh air again, his feet, as he could feel, were still trapped in the scrap of words. Günter Grass' *The Tin Drum*, which was to follow in 1959, also had such

an incredible impact because it was a signal—a drum roll—
to say that the linguistic repair work in German literature
would soon be completed and that here, once again, as had
always been the case elsewhere, writers would have all their
words at their disposal. That a new norm was beginning to
take effect. And if things weren't quite as ideal as that, they
at least appeared so, to our eyes.

And so German writers—and with them their colleagues
from Austria and Switzerland—can, it goes without saying,
again join the long line made up of your predecessors and
successors. We walk one behind the other, an interminably
long procession from sunrise to sunset. This rat's tail of a line
is what is called tradition, and you, at a place not of your own
choosing, are part of it. Everyone in the line puts their hand
on the shoulder of the person in front and feels on their own
shoulder the hand of the one walking behind.—Then at some
point, you, having aged meanwhile, are walking right at the
front of the living and behind the most recently deceased.
Not far ahead you see—yes, whom?—Robert Gernhardt,
still exactly as you recall him, and over there, Ernst Jandl
and Reinhard Lettau, and yes, indeed, Wolfgang Hildesheimer, who, now that he is dead, looks even more like Moses
than when alive. In front of them, a good bit ahead but still
recognizable—from behind, that is—Franz Kafka and
directly in front of him, Rainer Maria Rilke. Are the two
really chatting away cheerfully? A laughing Kafka, yes, that's
for sure—but a grinning Rilke?—Then, farther and farther
away, blacker and blacker, the eternal procession of those of

whom we know only one in every thousand, at best Georg Büchner, Heinrich von Kleist, yes, and the massive one there, who eats up so much space as he walks, has to be Johann Wolfgang von Goethe. — In front of him are, of course, others still, but most of these not even he sees, the Middle High German poet, perhaps, who kept a falcon for more than a year[2] or the ancient shaman from the area round Merseburg who, with his bone-to-bone Old High German incantations, tried to mend broken arms and legs.[3] Yes, really far up in front, the predecessors, the lines of writers and doctors, fuse into one another — the writers wanted to heal and the healers chanted magic words. — The hand on my shoulder could belong to Sarah Kirsch or, maybe, Elfriede Jelinek. You don't get to choose the man in front or the woman behind you. From time to time I, of course, turn my head, but looking back is awkward. Looking behind while walking forward, at my age, goes as well, or as badly, as reverse parking might. But I can see, not so far behind, those who are a shade younger. Him or her, I know. Then the young ones, whose hustle and bustle I sometimes get to know about, and finally, the really young who, so far behind me, all look pretty much the same. A strange tribe of Indians with unfamiliar customs. A few dance off to the side, again and again one disappears, abandons the line, because they're exhausted or have spotted a different path in life that appeals more.

Writing is now, in Germany, once again what it always was: a deviation from the norm. A different way of speaking, a hint different or very different. In saying that, the linguistic norm, of course, is neither static nor innocent. On the contrary, it is in constant motion and conveys all the lustre and dirt of history. It is so unpredictable and takes things into its own hands so much that even the most zealous reform commission — wishing merely to shoot down some new spelling and return to some good old spelling of a word — hasn't the slightest chance of influencing it in any way. Language does what it does. Someone or other adds something here. A part dies, barely noticed, there. It may be that the language of Goethe and Weimar Classicism still hasn't quite lost its function as a kind of standard metre for the German language. What is certain is: Goethe's way of speaking was not at all felt by his contemporaries to be automatically binding but, rather, a violation of *their* linguistic norm.

I am much tempted to say that *all* writers, in the emphatic sense of the word, deviate in that way from the language of those who define the largest common denominator. And they do so involuntarily. They would perhaps all like to speak like everyone else but can't. They can do what *they* can do. To write in a literary manner is not a voluntary decision, you're condemned to do so. It is a pressing necessity that — if the writing succeeds — can become a sort of second-degree happiness. Like Samuel Beckett being happy whenever he'd failed better again. Often, and for many, writing is a curse that only for us readers (and then a little, after all, for the writers themselves) can appear to be a blessing, since what was terrible and pressing has taken on form and structure.

Let me explain using the example of my fellow countryman Robert Walser, who, in my lifetime, has gone from being an absolute nobody to a classic of world literature. He knew very well that he wrote 'differently' but he could no other. That is where his quiet radicality stems from. It was the way *he* spoke. There is hardly a sentence by Walser that is congruent with the 'normal' way of speaking. Sometimes barely a hair separates the two. But the deviation is always there, the difference is irrevocable. Walser's texts do indeed have content—it would be possible to produce a conventional synopsis of *The Assistant*, for example—nonetheless, one can say with complete justification that Walser's actual content is the deviation, and not the story told as if in passing. It wasn't even as if he aimed for the differences—no, he made, *nolens volens*, a virtue of his necessity. He yearned greatly, on the contrary, for the normal, for a 'normal' way of speaking, but it was never possible for him. He took what he tended to experience as an *inability*—not being able to speak like the adults round him, whose feet were firmly planted in life—and regarded it, instead, as a *quality*. That was *his* stroke of genius. As he couldn't triumph like the many, with their language so confident of victory, he failed and celebrated his failure with a humble pride. With a relentless contrariness. He was at risk from the very beginning. How much he would've liked to be and to speak like all the others. And how precisely he recognized that he was unable to do exactly that.

As a result of his deviations, incidentally, Walser, who wrote so simply, apparently, is very difficult to translate. (That is true, *cum grano salis*, of all literature.) Only a writer, who — in his own language, that is, the target language — is a similarly sensitive kindred spirit, can translate him. I don't know whether or not Walser has found such a person. It is to be feared (this too is true of *all* literature) that his translators — heaving a sigh of relief because they understand the sentence in question — settle for the sense of the words and do without the message contained in the deviation, partly because they haven't even noticed it. Sometimes, it's really nothing more than a trembling of the palate; and a French palate, for example, trembles at very different frequencies. French, to speak only of that language, is much more 'ready' than German, is defined almost definitively and thus much less capable of the kind of deviation Walser takes for granted.

But even the reader lucky enough to speak German (and perhaps even capable of picking up on the Biel version of Bernese German that was Walser's mother tongue) can only understand Walser's texts if he is able, so to speak, to read with his third eye. With that free-floating attention that senses the deviations in every sentence. It is in the jittery and contrary differences from everyday speech that what Walser means emerges.

In saying that, Walser was certainly helped by the fact his writing grew from the margins. From a cultural margin that, simultaneously, was a linguistic margin. He lived for only a short time at the centre, in his Berlin period, and was perceived there for a few years as a droll, would-be writer. He was definitely successful, if by 'success' you mean he got to sit at the same table as the artists who set the tone in town, and that Kafka, who was even less well known, read him with enthusiasm in faraway Prague. But then fate forced him back to the margin he came from. He had indeed been born right on a linguistic border and never made a fuss—as it was self-evident—of the fact he could speak French. That is a book I should like to read: *The Walk*—*La promenade*—in Walser's own translation.

In the literatures of many languages, the inhabitants of border regions are often the most interesting people. Kafka in Czech Prague. Italo Svevo—with one foot in German—in Trieste. Danilo Kiš, who—all his (too short) life—didn't quite know whether he was Hungarian, Serbian or French. And Marguerite Duras' sparkling French certainly owes much to its roots in Indochina.

Sometimes, the language of writers shifts away from the norm so violently (for instance, late Hölderlin) that the bridges of communication are torn down. Then the text is 'mad' and the writer too, who can't say things any differently. Things didn't ever go that far with Walser, although the deviation—in *The Robber* or in the late micrograms—becomes greater. *The Robber* is possibly the only novel in the history of literature to have been written without a single thought of any possible reader. It's a text that has so radically given up all hope of any echo that Walser didn't ever consider making a fair copy from his illegible scraps of paper. Writing itself was enough for him; had to be, given the icily seething solitude that had then, once and for all, become his fate.

No one is free to choose his linguistic fate. The writers' own, often so wondrous linguistic possibilities are also the prison that they are locked up in. For life. However brilliant the language area commanded by the individual writer might look, it has limits that everyone faces. No escape possible. Schiller couldn't do what Goethe did, and Goethe couldn't do what Schiller did. No one can do what someone else can, not these days either. Arnold Stadler can't do what Gert Jonke does, but nor can Gert Jonke do what Arnold Stadler does. Isn't that marvellous? For that reason too, there is no patent office for poetry, because no writer's work can be stolen. Those writers who really became one-offs— Büchner, Kleist, Kafka—have no successors for that reason. Merely imitators. But imitators write, in the manner of their model, in a *dead* way—whereas the model vibrated with life.

The prison cells of most writers tend to be small; we don't love them any less for that. Goethe overwhelmed us in the way he did because, truly a Proteus, he lived in a complex with so many rooms and gardens that it almost seemed as if he were living in liberty. Walser had a harder time of it, no doubt. He couldn't stage his deviations from the norm of the many as brilliantly as the man from Frankfurt in Weimar. On the contrary, in his case, readers often had the fatal feeling in the present they shared, the here and now, that they too could do that, write something as ordinary as that. It often looked like something anyone could do. That everyone thought they could do, just as once there were people who thought an ape could draw like Picasso, and every child, for sure. That no one could do what Walser could in such matter-of-fact fashion only our generation—with a few honourable exceptions, Walter Benjamin first and foremost—noticed. His contemporaries hadn't realized—how could they have?—that Walser was fighting, in the form of his little trifles, for his life and, soon, could no longer summon the strength to face his demons, the daily and, even more so, *nightly* panic, and had withdrawn to psychiatry to the Waldau in Berne initially and then reluctantly to Herisau. He was happy in the institution, happy in his own way, as he now no longer had to write. He left his demons in peace so they would leave him in peace, and worked—without writing anything and with a minimum of spoken words—on his disappearance with that unique radicality of his, gentle and humble and, in short outbursts, with a violent temper. By the time he died in 1956, he'd disappeared so successfully that I, though of age by then—but still without a driving licence— and aware of Walser's not yet completely faded local fame, didn't notice his passing at all. Couldn't my father have said at the dinner table, 'Son, Walser died today'? But he didn't because he'd heard nothing either about the death of the most touching writer from my home country in the twentieth century. It was, after all, also Christmas at the time.

The deviations from general speech, whether greater or lesser, that can be traced in all writing, permit us to sense the tensions to which everyone who writes is exposed. With as clear a view as possible, you must face up to the deviation, the difference, must endure it and give it the form to which it is most suited; and yet, you are not permitted to be carried off course, to that place where communication ceases and occasional madness begins. It's easy to become a writer. It's difficult to remain one. To set off, again and again, for those regions that—for you, in any case—are life-threatening, and then, having managed to round things off, to return undamaged.

Those who swim with the mainstream do so for self-protection rather than for tactical reasons. The *main* stream —Frankfurt is on the Main, as you know—has something very pleasant; you can let yourself drift on familiar words that, even if they sound important and powerful, don't hurt. Mainstream books aren't evil either, each and every one of us swims along, every now and then, for a few hundred metres. Conformity is necessary for survival, and learning a language—that will then be the material for your art—is certainly not part of a process of individuation, rather, the attempt to do things as everyone else does. I say dog, you understand dog; at most, yours looks like a chow, and mine like a Doberman Pinscher. In an ideal world—let's call it Paradise—every word would be a glitteringly clear concept, no ambivalence for miles round, no dyed-black subtext standing in contradiction to what was said openly, no hint of any hidden meaning. The lion asks the lamb the time and the latter answers, without malice, it's the eleventh hour. Maybe Paradise would be a little boring for people like you and me but as no one would actually think that way, it wouldn't matter. Maybe God was indeed a little bored with his Paradise back then and, mischievously, put it to the test. A little experiment, not really important, God would also have accepted Eve ignoring his snake in Eden. In an ideal and, clearly, eternal Paradise, in any case, only books—if at all— of a blissfully mainstream nature would be written, that is, those brightly lit stories in which naked women lie beside naked men, without beginning to think of an apple, without beginning to think at all. In unambivalent zones, thoughts are not had. That's why in our real world too, very kind people, on the one hand—founders of religions, gurus—and the dictators, on the other, always create linguistic clarities. In Paradise and in dictatorships, there is no poetry. Only hymns of praise. Poetry is resistant for that reason alone: it is defined by differences.

And nowadays? The free market economy that has become power-hungry, indeed, gone raving mad in the years since 1989, that no longer appreciates being called capitalism, is demonstrating more and more clearly a will for a language that would be obligatory for as many people as possible. For a jargon that—although it consists almost exclusively of euphemisms—feigns unambiguity. Everything defined in crystal-clear fashion, even if it contradicts reality most glaringly. In 'free market economy', the word 'free' is already the first example. Those who speak the jargon of the new economy are revealing their wish to be among the victors. Part of the one-third of society that tells the other two-thirds what's what. If you stick to the words themselves, it's often just funny, and I often ask myself, when present at victors' conversations, why the speakers don't blush with shame or burst into hellish laughter. Here, chosen at random, are job adverts from a single edition of the *Neue Zürcher Zeitung*, a German-language newspaper, incidentally. There is an advert, for example, for a 'Corporate Key Relationship Manager'—using the English term—with, I quote, 'a natural affinity for transatlantic communication styles and an intercultural all-round education'. There are adverts too—again using these English terms—for a 'Vice President Corporate Staff Management Resources', a 'Change Manager', a 'Manager Component Purchasing and Subcontracting', a 'Business Process Engineer', an 'Area Sales Manager', an 'Event Coordinator', a 'Human Resources Consultant', a 'Chief Executive Officer', an 'Integration Manager Supplier', a 'Supply Chain Manager', a 'Procurement Officer', a 'Senior Consultant', a 'Head of Operations' and a 'Deal Manager'.—Of course, it's clear to all of us that many old and familiar activities are being revamped with splendid-sounding job titles. The 'Area Sales Manager' will no doubt, as ever, set off with his vacuum cleaners and get the door slammed in his face by unwilling housewives. And isn't a 'Manager Component Purchasing and Subcontracting' simply a good old bookkeeper, with or without the elbow patches?

With the language of the increasingly globalized economy, ideals are being drummed into us that we are supposed to take at face value. And many people do, for it is not only love that is blind but also the ambition to be among the victors. Speaking the language of the victors, one becomes clear oneself, unambiguous. And that the words used erect—sentence by sentence—a linguistic facade, a sham, isn't a problem as long as your opposite number fiddles about with props from the same store. The victors' values are good, as are their words, there are absolutely no others. There is, once again, no this-as-well-as-that. There is, once again, no ambivalence. Haven't the hard men of the past become the cool guys of today? And don't the modern-day alpha males jogging so bitterly through the park at six in the morning make you begin to suspect that these healthy, competitive people might very well regard the not-so-healthy and less competitive as some kind of worthless life? Isn't the *Kraft* of the past just like *power* nowadays? And isn't the *efficiency* we know today somehow similar to that *will* in the past that had to win through at any price? Military thinking and military language are ever present, at any rate, in the new economy. War in a made-to-measure suit. Large firms are made up of *divisions*, and even the baker on the corner says, if he helps out at the counter, that he's in the *front line*. Those representing the values of the economy turn very aggressively against everything that deviates from the norms. From their norms.

A new jargon has established itself, the pre-fascist connotations of which cannot be denied. Either way, I'm amazed by how little we are generally conscious of the glaring contradiction that shapes our daily lives. Namely, we see ourselves as politically mature democrats and resist, with good reason, any reduction of our democratic rights. We permit our politicians not even the slightest hint of self-aggrandizement. Woe betide them if they don't ask for permission to patch the roof of the art gallery. At the same time, we take ourselves daily into a world of work where very little is arranged democratically. The boss is right, even when he's wrong, and, at times, we are this boss. How can we actually endure this without going mad—by day, receiving and passing on instructions, in keeping with one's defined function, and in the evening, being a mature citizen, equally concerned about the welfare of everyone? —The language of the economy has the task, inter alia, of hallucinating this pressure away. If no contradictions are identified, if none *can* be identified, there cannot be any.

And so, perhaps, a circle begins to close, that spiral, rather, in which we've been operating since 1945. Once again, we are confronted with sham language that is only interested in power and that could do, again, with having an axe taken to it, that is, another *Kahlschlag*. Could do with people who, like in Aichinger's book, would try to unlearn it instead of acquiring it. We hear the inauthentic jargon of power daily and we speak it from time to time, no doubt. But those of us writing today—young and old—can't be accused of falling meekly into the traps set by the language of economic life. No. Perhaps, on the contrary, nowadays too, writers are, for language, something like what earthworms are for the ground. They keep it nice and loose—thus ensuring something can grow and flourish.

So not their *language*. It's probably too dull and boring for any writer to adopt naively, on a scale of one to one. As his own, and only, way of speaking. The secret and open *ideals* of our times *do*, however, affect us. All too often, we take the lead in embracing those perversions that, for many people, already appear to be normal. How many of us are fascinated by violence, by coldness. How many of us celebrate death and not life.—More about that, and a few other things, later.

Thank you.

On the Suffering of Writers

Ladies and Gentlemen,

Last Tuesday, I spoke about the deviation from the linguistic norm that makes poetry poetry. Today, I'm going to give the same lecture again—okay, maybe not in the same words—and shall call that deviation suffering. I wish to speak about the suffering of writers. For without suffering, without pain, literature doesn't happen.

A warning, however, to begin with: don't believe anyone who tries to tell you that writing—as in, the act of writing—is terrible. Or torture. The opposite is true. Writing, when it succeeds, is the most splendid thing that can happen to you. It is sheer joy. It is just that writing that succeeds doesn't always happen, like a successful life doesn't happen every day. Writers who complain about it don't actually mean writing. They mean not-writing. Not being able to write, that hurts. And the points of intersection—where having-to-write and not-being-able-to-write clash—are certainly painful.

Let's begin with the most obvious form of suffering. Madness. You know the old joke: what's the one difference between an artist and a madman? The artist isn't mad. That *is* a joke but I quote it anyway since—precisely because of its tautological nature—it contains a good piece of truth. The proximity of the artist, in general, and the writer, in particular, to madness is something we're familiar with from the publications of Cesare Lombroso and Wilhelm Lange-Eichbaum. Torquato Tasso, J. M. R. Lenz, Friedrich Hölderlin, Nikolaus Lenau, Gérard de Nerval, Nikolai Gogol, Guy de Maupassant, Conrad Ferdinand Meyer, Friedrich Nietzsche, August Strindberg—the list of writers who were truly swallowed up by their suffering is movingly long. Every writer comes into contact with suffering—mental problems, first and foremost—such that we are amazed at how many equally talented colleagues were, and are, capable of leading a steady, autonomous, vigorous life. Mainly at the cost of violent struggles with themselves, that's for sure. A wrestling match, from which the healthy part of them did emerge victorious, after all. Goethe, Büchner, Chekhov managed to stay on this side of the line that separates us from the voracious whirlpool of mental health imperilment. Shakespeare too—a genius when it came to illuminating human delusions—was 'normal', if we wish to regard the instruction in his will to give his wife the 'second-best bed', and nothing but that, as normal. At any rate, talent, even genius, is certainly not *necessarily* linked to some form of madness. There are highly talented, and untalented, mad people just as there are ingenious and talentless individuals among those who are capable of living a life of conformity.

If I wish, therefore, to say something about the suffering of writers, then it is above all about how they, *by writing*, face up to suffering—their own and that of others. Also, and *especially*, in literature there isn't *one* ideal way—many roads lead to Rome, if not, of course, all roads. Every writer handles pain in life differently. Every single one, however, has to deal with suffering. The background to and the impetus for *all* literary writing is a form of suffering, a blind nucleus, in which the writing—something the writer can't express conceptually—is concealed, in a highly concentrated form and ready to explode. The writer can't voice his suffering because he doesn't know it—at least, not in *exact detail*—and yet he *has* to voice it because the pain would tear him apart were he to remain silent. Every writer has to make confessions to his readers, the content of which he, at best, can sense but never precisely label. In all writing that merits the name, there is an energy that is fed by a suffering, a suffering that is difficult to master; an energy that lives, somewhere beyond crystal-clear concepts, within the artists.—However, suffering alone doesn't guarantee good writing. Books along the lines of 'I'm not feeling especially well today and I'll now tell you why' exist in considerable numbers, it's true, but they are hardly ever works of art. In art, alongside the suffering that is always accumulated involuntarily, and alongside one's own deficit, there needs to be a surplus that is just as great. Strength, the urge to play, hope in life, utopia. Without this force of a godlike desire to create, nothing comes into being and so, the writing of the great tragic poets — also, or *especially* — has a mighty, utopian surplus. Art creates life, not death, and anyone who wishes to create life must know a great deal about *life*. That art, for that very reason, always speaks of death too — it refuses to accept death, tries to ward it off — has to do with art's life-giving aspirations.

Literature is in search of insight. It wants to know and — by nature — wishes, first of all, to track down suffering and the reasons for it. The only thing is that this search for insight is always hindered — now more forcefully, now less so — by its antithesis. Which is to say, literature is also the denial of this insight, such that the poetic result — not at all to its detriment, for this ambivalence is part of literature — is a kind of draw, a zero-sum game, a hovering between insight and its denial that leaves a lot of leeway for our interpretation. *Our* interpretation. For the writer doesn't get any further than he has come with his text, and is often the last person to spot the solution. *The* solution, that's wrong too. For a literary text, there is never a single key that will unlock all its secrets for us. Literature isn't a crossword.

I've already spoken — fifteen years ago, in my Lectures on Poetics in Graz — about how, from time to time, I imagine an ideal landscape where writers, and only writers, live. I've never stopped fantasizing about this landscape — somewhere in it, I reside too, after all — and would like to paint it again for you. In this landscape, like everywhere else, a colossal lot has been built and we've become more mobile. Nevertheless. The country is still a vast plain, or if there are any hills, they, at least, still allow us to see all the way to the farthest end. In the foreground, the plain is in brilliant, bright sunlight; further back, it darkens gradually to a black horizon. Somewhere in this flat country, everyone has his or her house. In the brightness, where we are, live many people; and there's quite a bit of tussling and jostling. Sometimes, one of us bravely walks in the direction of the blackness for an hour or two but then turns back in time, not wishing, or unable, to remain with those more uncertain people already living in the more broken light. Right at the edge, at the point where a steep cliff drops into a raging black abyss, only the bold and the condemned have their homes. Walser—as you can guess from what I've said—lives here, his house is still next door to Hölderlin's, but the two haven't seen each other in the past fifteen years (neither has ever seen what the other sees). For Walser's window still only ever points towards the light. He stands there looking, with all the strength he can muster, out of the blackness— behind him rages the abyss—across to the normal that he can just about distinguish in the distance. Hölderlin, in contrast, has his window, as ever, on the other side of his house and looks out into the menace. Into the abyss. —That area isn't very populated. The climate, after all, is also *very* inhospitable, even for those poets who aren't put out by a downpour. Tasso lives there, Edgar Allan Poe, E. T. A.

Hoffmann, and that there, in the distance, could be the home of Adalbert Stifter. Goethe, it goes without saying, also has a hut here, for emergencies; but then he has a dwelling in every part of the landscape. — Kafka. Where does Kafka live? He doesn't have a house at all any more. He has jumped over the edge of the abyss, into the black void, and is writing in free fall.

Of course, such a description is a metaphor. I could also have expressed the findings in more conceptual terms. But the metaphorical is indeed the domain of literature, precisely because writers can't capture the core of their pain with concepts and, therefore, explore it again and again, from different angles. They get closer and closer, right up to the pain threshold and beyond. Then withdraw and formulate their findings, which, of necessity, must remain provisional. Such findings *can* be formulated only metaphorically, a confession in the form of images; they don't push forward in a bid to arrive at the concept. That is *not* a deficit of literature, but the only way in uncharted terrain, nonetheless, to arrive at insights. Literature — its most serious examples — resides where science cannot — not yet — because it lacks the instruments, the concepts. Literature scans still dark spaces, using metaphor. Insight triumphs when the crystal-clear concept is found and that is the goal and domain of exact science.

That literature works with metaphor — a story in place of a concept — is not a licence for arbitrariness. Literature, which is allowed to do everything, isn't allowed to do this because nothing matters anyway. It must, on the contrary, if it wishes to remain abreast of its times and its own necessity, assimilate the world of concepts and reside in an uncharted place that others haven't long since illuminated. Of course, it occasionally often lumbers round in landscapes long since charted by others. Not every writer is so radical in each of his works that he dares to reside exclusively in the most dangerous regions.—Metaphor, then, in order to capture suffering more precisely. Metaphor, incidentally, is not unknown to the sciences that are labelled exact. Often, they have to work with it too, because nothing better is available. The term 'schizophrenia', for example, if I understand correctly, has remained until this day a metaphor, retracted to a single word; a metaphor that doesn't reach beyond an initial summary understanding. And physics, too, has its unproved propositions, with which it fiddles round as if they were true.

The writer who suffers creates his works because without these confessions he'd implode—the gods have shown him mercy in permitting him this possibility; and *also* because a positive reception helps to integrate him into the community. Suffering, famously, isolates people and the— perhaps even enthusiastic—acceptance of his black confessions allows the writer to see that these black confessions cannot be entirely foreign to the readers. For the writer arrives every day anew at the banal insight that being wounded really does hurt. In order not to be swamped by the pain, he is forced to create distance, distance between himself and the material, and distance between himself and the reader. *No* writing—I know this experience is my equivalent of *ceterum censeo*—ever just suddenly emerges, straight out of seething emotions. On the contrary, during the process of writing the seething emotions—of necessity—transform into a concentrated observation of the material and, in the end, can barely be felt by the writer. As if a sheet of glass were between them and him. The writing even of the most terrible thing, *especially* of the most terrible thing, happens in an oddly cold fashion. Were we to feel exactly what we write or want to write, we wouldn't be able to do it. The pain would tear us apart and we wouldn't write another word. Yes, it is even the case that the feeling experienced while writing is often the diametrical opposite of that in the text. I describe a painful death and the feeling while writing is not of mourning but joy. Triumph. In Walter Muschg's words: 'The most wonderful sheen on a masterpiece is the pain that no longer pains the author. A perfect piece of work must no longer bear a single trace of the suffering.'[4]

This apparent faulty circuit—pleasure instead of pain—stems from the fact that, internally, the writer is celebrating the victory of form over content. The readers then celebrate with him because they co-write in their heads while reading. Literature comes into being at that moment in which life—unlimited, diffuse—takes on structure. This aesthetic victory triggers incredible relief; it is a triumph over evil life, even if evil life still continues.

I believe we are all, even outside literature, very often and very intensely busy keeping the fears in check that go hand in hand with life. Exaggerating a little, one can say we do *everything* we can to try and introduce stable structures to the chaos. For example, we can content ourselves with almost every explanation if its structure and form appear strong enough to contain fear. Whether the explanation is correct isn't as important. This applies to literature and it applies to the sciences too. How many axioms that looked like the ultimate truth proved one day to be provisional! Their so convincing structure, however, had seduced our forefathers into seeing them as chapter and verse; the solution. 'Eppur si muove,' Galileo said when the Inquisition held the knife to his throat and demanded a clear position on Copernicus' new interpretation of the structure of the universe. Man, too, was just an ape, said Darwin. And Freud tried to teach us that man isn't even the master in his own house. These are the three famous mortifications of humanity, and to accept them we had to abandon, each time, notions that were very effective when it came to confining fear. That the universe is Earth-centred. That God created man. And that we make our decisions exactly as we wish. It wasn't easy, deciding to do without such wonderfully calming notions and no one in this room, I imagine, is entirely free of them, even now. I am already trembling at the thought of learning what the fourth mortification will be, which will force us to abandon all those notions that helped us confine fear, quite simply because the strength of evidence, the obviousness of the new thought, is too powerful. I fear the fourth mortification is already blazing on all our walls, *mene mene tekel*, and will say that we humans, in so and so many years, will have vanished from the earth. Not a large number of years: ten, one hundred or two hundred. The lifetime of your grandchildren, maybe. What is now an inkling, or murmuring, will be proved indisputably, to many, many digits after the decimal point.

I can hardly speak about suffering, the suffering of writers, without trying to describe the impact of Freud on what we do. He unsettled the writers of his time to the extreme—he still unsettles many today—and forced them all to deal differently with what they regarded as their very own: knowledge of the human soul. For, from the ancient Greeks onwards, and in increasingly nuanced fashion, writers had known how to capture the human heart and its stirrings poetically; that is, metaphorically; writers up to and including Freud's writing contemporaries, of whom Chekhov was perhaps the most talented. He, the same age as Freud, 'knew' everything that Freud 'knew'. The difference was 'only' that Freud systematized this knowledge and harnessed it for science. That wasn't, and isn't, *better*. It was a different aim. He then used—and not by chance—the work of *writers* as a source for the concepts he formulated. Sophocles, Shakespeare, Dostoevsky. Not better, but something different. Nonetheless, the world with and after Freud looked different from the one before him. Above all, there was no avoiding his research becoming an almost intolerable mortification for the writers of his time. For until that point, the description and interpretation of human feelings had been *their* domain. It was *they* who knew about the storms of the heart. About the unconscious, which they were tracing, even if they weren't yet able to label it. Freud must have seemed like someone poaching round a preserve that was theirs, and only theirs. Many writers also resented him for it—Joseph Conrad, for instance. André Breton, Vladimir Nabokov, Elias Canetti— and not only them—were aggressive and dismissive towards Freud all their lives, although—or precisely, *because*—they had no real idea about what mattered to him. Chekhov wasn't. He didn't know him—just as Freud didn't know Chekhov—and so he's also the last and greatest of those writers who wrote before, and without, Freud. Pity, the two never met. I sometimes have the impression that Chekhov, the doctor, wasn't so very far away from a classification of human behaviour. His plays can be read as a kind of test assembly.

Naturally, no one writing nowadays can ignore Freud's insights. Which doesn't alter the fact—at most, makes everything more difficult—that poetry, unlike science, lives off the blessing of naivety. The space in which poetry moves can only be entered naively. But a writer who wishes to write consistently, and indispensably, must never *feign* naivety. He must *be* naive—although, or precisely *because*, he doesn't dodge knowing about the world. Naive, but with a keen hunger for knowledge: that's trying to square the circle, almost. That said, it is very much possible that his naivety is fed and protected by that blind nucleus of pain, by the encapsulated trauma that emits its wild impulses and yearns for liberation. Naivety, nevertheless, is not simply defence or, as the case may be, successful repression. It is characterized by an optimistic curiosity and love of playing that elevate it beyond that.

Freud shifted the boundaries regarding this naivety such that the methods used by Chekhov or, if you like, Dostoevsky, or even Arthur Schnitzler, to capture the human heart and its stirrings, were no longer available to the writers who came after him. The writers now *knew* too, and inescapably so. What to do? Where were the new methods with which to get to grips with suffering? (Which hadn't, of course, vanished from the earth.) Methods that would again permit the naivety, without which creativity seems impossible? (Of course, it wasn't only Freud who smashed the entire aesthetics of the late nineteenth century to pieces. There were other factors too, including a world war.) There were many attempts, Dada, the surrealists, James Joyce. I'd like to single out Joyce's secretary, Beckett. For his work and for us, he created an impressive new naive space that knew about Freud's main insight—the unconscious—and yet was a *terra incognita* on which he was now the first to walk. As the days of Chekhov-style naivety were now over, Beckett first had to find out where the boundaries could be redrawn. So he acted stupid and pretended not to care at all about psychology. The opposite, of course, was the case. While pretending to vacate the space occupied by psychology—by letting his heroes perform their simple, often almost childish-seeming games—he re-entered it, initially unnoticed by us, through the back door. With us yet—at all—to understand what he was actually doing, he took Chekhov's heroes apart, reduced them to pieces and put them together again, differently and fragmentarily. He showed us just parts of ourselves—now this, now that—and looked, through the surface, directly into the unconscious. In *Waiting for Godot*, it seems as if the—unfiltered— unconscious itself becomes a scene. Estragon, Vladimir, Pozzo and Lucky appear to be agents of *a single* unconscious, not four 'characters' in the sense of the previous psychological theatre. Nowadays (because we understand better), it seems even more admirable than it did back then how radical and courageous Beckett was in illuminating areas that 'normally' are so fear-laden that we avert them and do not even begin to attach language to them. Beckett's technique, his way of demonstrating the radically illogical inter- connectedness of the unconscious, was labelled absurd. Absurd theatre: that was a theatre beyond the laws of the real. Nowadays, with us knowing more about the (indeed) absurd capers of the unconscious and these things therefore being more self-evident and less frightening, Beckett's psychology seems like pure realism. We understand, easily. Estragon and Vladimir feel and think as we do, which is to say, they are thought and felt. As we are. They are marionettes that fidget round at the end of strings pulled by the unconscious. Beckett is Chekhov after Freud even if, or precisely because, he turns Chekhov's method on its head. Appears to disallow psychology at the very places where Chekhov is incredibly nuanced. His best works, like those of Chekhov, have that aura of necessity that distinguishes all great literature. You don't contradict a tree, a downpour or a mountain. Nor do you contradict either *Waiting for Godot* or *Uncle Vanya*.

Many arrive, via their suffering, at texts of a depth that would be unthinkable without such a potent nucleus of pain. In many cases, successfully expressing what was threatening to the author may lead even to a kind of 'healing'. Famously, one realizes one has solved a problem when the problem disappears. And during a writing life, many an affliction is perhaps overcome precisely by writing about it. The fortunate may succeed in that. Despite that, I would never recommend writing as therapy to anyone. For, many people can no longer manage—especially when the years begin to pass and their originally abundant strength begins to fade—to face up to their pain as forcefully and aggressively as before, that is, with that combination of decisive confrontation and clear distance that makes expressing it possible. They react in very different ways. In defeat, too, there's not merely *one* road out of Rome and it's different from the one that once led you *in*. Some, in their writing, try to dodge pain by sticking to what is harmless and prattling on, using sophisticated techniques acquired in the course of their writing lives. Others fake it, expressing a pain, but ending up some distance from their own. Many retreat to irony. By no means a few tie themselves down, once and for all, to their particular view of the world—their interpretation of reality fossilizes—and they're then offended when life contradicts them.

The most radical reaction is to fall silent. Many, especially of the greats, came to know painfully long periods of silence. And many stopped writing completely as, at some point, it proved to be the wrong way or one they could no longer take. Goethe, known for preferring to write about the contours of clouds or the shape of petals than not to write at all, nonetheless had long periods of silence. Schiller, Lenau, Kleist, Stifter. Gottfried Keller. Shakespeare, too, suddenly stopped—after an apotheosis of stormy feelings that he rightly called *The Tempest*—and retreated to Stratford-upon-Avon. The most conspicuously silent writer I know is Arthur Rimbaud, of whom Henry Miller—who knew about these things—reportedly said he was the unhappiest person who ever lived. Rimbaud stopped writing at the age of twenty and, in his remaining seventeen years, didn't only not write another literary word but he was never again to comment— never, in the real sense of the word—on any aesthetic matter. Only on everyday things and his problems as a merchant. And I must admit: to me, this muffled radicality makes his period of silence down in the hellish heat of Aden just as fascinating as the period in which he wrote.

Denying dangerous pain becomes more and more difficult as the years pass because the naivety and innocence that can perhaps be found in one's early work fade as one's writing age increases. It's not as if the writer *only* gropes round in the fogs of his cluelessness. He understands very well a part of what he is doing. This part does hurt; the part to which one remains blind, even more so. A few years ago, Hildesheimer announced—almost as a manifesto—that he'd never write another literary text. He withdrew to painting, worked on his collages and explicitly justified this decision by suggesting that this form of artistic activity made it easier for him to resist the now intolerable pain and, unlike words, didn't reopen wounds that hadn't healed sufficiently.

That is *a* solution. That is *not* a solution. I fear one doesn't choose when it is one stops. It might even be that we *are* stopped, all together, all at once. Émile Cioran voiced, three decades ago already, something that then on the whole seemed eccentric and that, now, seems to be almost what everyone thinks: 'In permitting man, Nature has committed much more than a mistake in her calculations: a crime against herself.'[5] And so, that same Nature—right at this moment—is possibly in the process of correcting its mistake and of getting rid of us. Nature strikes back—in happier times, only the Empire did that—and when we human beings have gone, Nature will still be the same: changing, patient, unfeeling.

Nowadays, apocalyptic thinking is almost, as it were, common property, and not only in the case of writers. The Apocalypse, no longer a metaphor, is in the process of becoming a predictable factor. Once we're up to our neck in the waters of the melting polar ice caps, we'll long for the hideous beauty of the four horsemen on their horses: the first horse, white; the second, red; the third, black; the fourth, sallow; and the person sitting on it—his name is Death. How beautiful, this image is! Especially, since the horsemen are on the horizon and not in our midst, not yet. The image is not just terrible, it's also seductive—like all images that simulate terror in such a way that we get to experience it on a trial basis and not perish in the process. The Apocalypse is, for that reason, an attractive option: on the last day *everyone* dies, you too, not only me, alone and barely noticed by any of those who remain alive for the moment.

Existential pessimism—the kind also that, like that of Cioran or, again, Beckett, has largely been divested of its Christian connotations and manages entirely without a god—is certainly older than our current ecological problems. It is more than a reaction to the growing political threats that—to use Peter Sloterdijk's phrase—the almost immeasurable reservoir of rage that is Islamic fundamentalism holds for us.[6] It has been something like the basic configuration of writers from the beginning of time, becoming more manifest in one writer, less in others. Joseph Conrad, who in real life was politically abstinent or, rather, a loyal British Royalist, expressed this, in the century before last, thus:

> Man is a vicious animal. His viciousness must be organized. Crime is a necessary condition of organized existence. Society is essentially criminal—

or it would not exist. Selfishness preserves every-thing—absolutely everything—everything we hate and everything we love. And everything holds together. That is why I respect the extreme anar-chists. 'I hope for general extermination.' Very well. It's justifiable and, moreover, it is plain. One compromises with words. There's no end to it. It's like a forest where no one knows the way. One is lost even as one is calling out 'I am saved!'[7]

So-called modernism, for which many a definition has been suggested, can probably be captured with those last two sentences.

Because, nowadays, we agree quite naturally with this view (does that make us postmodern?), those modernist works—that, at the time of their creation, were considered inaccessible—have likewise, in the meantime, become more comprehensible. In 1951, *Waiting for Godot* was an unsettling puzzle because it presupposed and took for granted the inescapability of Conrad's sentence, whereas we were still clinging to life models that seemed to offer us a let-out and so were easier to bear. Nowadays, we are all much less likely to dismiss Beckett's view of life, even if, taken literally, it is devastatingly fatal—or it simply, as happened to the genius himself, tips over into a fatalistically creative form of gallows humour, a fabulous joke beneath the gallows that repeatedly makes his play look as if Eugene Marin Labiche had whispered the dialogues into his ear. It's true that if one's view of the world is as grim as Beckett's, only despair or laughter remain. Beckett knew both. One can, I think, even stage pieces like *Krapp's Last Tape* —which is only ever staged, as far as I know, as a dark play about the end of everything —as a last piece of slapstick: farce instead of tragedy, with the very same script.

Those of us alive today needed a generation longer than Beckett to accept that we grope round blindly in the undergrowth of history, shouting 'We are saved,' whereas — in fact —we are long since lost. Tellingly, it is Pozzo, the anything but intellectual power-seeker, who utters Beckett's most personal creed: 'They' —women —'give birth astride of a grave, the light gleams an instant, then it's night once more.'[8] This gleam of light is our life.

Wolfgang Hildesheimer comes back to mind. Once when a natural catastrophe hit Poschiavo, where he lived, the village stream, from one minute to the next, rapidly became a bringer-of-ill-luck; tree trunks, cars and cows were soon being swept along, and because Wolfgang's house was the first to block the water's path, it tore with all its force through the entire ground floor, in through the front door and the windows; and out again at the back, before heading —now tree-less, car-less and cow-less again —down into the valley; and Wolfgang was standing in his pyjamas (it was well after midnight) on the first-floor balcony, shaking his fists and roaring into the chaos —yes, now it had come, doomsday had come, quite right, quite right, hadn't he said so all along. —That's the story as he told it to me, anyway, his prophetic anger still aglow. And if he didn't really shout out like that, he surely wanted to. It goes without saying that I loved, and love, him for it.

Yes. Everyone stops, at some point, somehow. Beckett demonstrated becoming silent over a period of years, in play after play, until these consisted only of silence and a few words here and there. Goethe, who was very different, wrote right up to his last day, or just about, and did so as part of a defiant aspiration to survive. Nowadays, not even the weightiest minds would dare to take a leaf from his book. 'If I work incessantly to the last,' he said, 'nature owes me another form of existence'.[9] Gosh! Let's hope that Nature has kept her promise.

The greatest panic of many — I mean me — is that the head, while the flesh is still willing, could stop functioning as it should. Not everyone anticipates his future and his end as accurately — as touchingly and frighteningly accurately — as Walser did nineteen years before he fell silent and forty-seven years before he died.

> Perhaps I shall never put out twigs and branches. One day some fragrance or other will issue from my nature and my originating, I shall flower, and the fragrance will shed itself around a little, then I shall bow my head [. . .] My arms and legs will strangely sag, my mind, pride, and character, everything will crack and fade, and I shall be dead, not really dead, only dead in a certain sort of way, and then I shall vegetate and die.[10]

And so it came to pass. Exactly like that. And in a short sketch, 'Eine Weihnachtsgeschichte', he even predicted his death in such exact detail that one could almost believe in prophecy. On which day—25 December; under which circumstances—a lonely walk in the snow; and even the coat and the hat that he wore on 25 December 1956, he described in the text written in 1919.

It's a comfort, at least, that everything—even those that we anticipate so carefully—turns out to be different still for us mere mortals. Maybe what simply stops is what the psychoanalysts call 'cathexis'. It simply no longer interests you. You no longer care about your stories, other people's stories. Death is: no longer wanting to hear and tell stories.

On the Dream of Singing Anonymously
in the Voice of the People

Ladies and Gentlemen,

Compared to German Literature—*The Song of the Nibelungs*, Walther von der Vogelweide, Hans Jakob Grimmelshausen—the literature of my homeland, Switzerland, is nothing less than in its infancy. At first nothing; then a little; barely anything throughout all of Middle Ages—it's supposed that Hartmann von Aue came from Eglisau but not even that is certain; then a few chronicles in the sixteenth century; like a monolith, the shepherd boy who was to become a scholar, Thomas Platter; and, not until the eighteenth century, a few more vigorous stirrings when it comes to literary writing. First and foremost, the incomparable rustic dilettante Ulrich Bräker; or little masters—also of pastoral poetry—like Johann Gaudenz von Salis-Seewis. In 1732, Albrecht von Haller laid the foundations of Swiss tourism with his long poem 'The Alps' because he was the first to see our bergschrunds, rock faces, glaciers and peaks as an aesthetic phenomenon and not something that stood in your way, and chucked stones and avalanches down on you, and that people, otherwise, did not even ignore. Before Haller, no Swiss person (or anyone at all, for that matter) would have called a mountaintop beautiful. Or even scaled it. (Petrarch was not Swiss and his ascent of Mont Ventoux—for the Swiss, a fairly high hill— was regarded as so whacky back then that, even in his world, no one understood why he'd done it. Yes, it was supposed— and is, to this day—that he simply invented the whole expedition. Probably wrongly.) In 1756, Salomon Gessner wrote the first best-seller to come out of Switzerland. His idylls were read by the whole of Europe. And Bodmer and Breitinger, both Johann Jakob, managed to attract Friedrich Klopstock, Christoph Martin Wieland and Johann Wolfgang von Goethe as admiring visitors to Zurich. They were passionate lovers of, and wordy agitators for, a literature of deep emotions and yet were two signposts who were, themselves, incapable of going in the direction they showed.

With the consequence that Switzerland did not gain a literature of its own until the nineteenth century. In the shape of both Jeremias Gotthelf, who, though he enjoys some kind of 'polite' success, remains, to this day, grossly underestimated, and Gottfried Keller. For their contemporaries in Zurich and Berne, these two emerged—so to speak—from nowhere, even if Keller and Gotthelf, themselves, knew precisely what they had German Literature to thank for. Keller insisted, positively defiantly, that he was a *German* writer and Gotthelf published his books with Julius Springer in Berlin. Round them, as before, hardly anyone who wrote even anywhere nearly as well. Who wrote at all. In Gotthelf's case, in the Emmen Valley, many couldn't even *read* his books. — Today, only a hundred and fifty years later, there are so many of us, so many proper writers in Switzerland, that we too can easily put together a national team with first-class subs on the bench. And the team qualifies, meanwhile, for all the important international tournaments: the European Championship, the World Cup. Only when it comes to the Nobel Prize do we always go out in the first round. — I can't tell you anything about the line-up, unfortunately, I am not the manager, after all. I'm a player, a regular; currently an attacking midfielder. The manager is Peter von Matt, and if I open my big gob too much, he takes me off before the end, and sends on one of the younger stars, Raphael Urweider, for instance, or Peter Stamm.

I'm going to do wrong by Gotthelf now too as I'd like to devote this hour to Keller — and for a special reason. *One* desire drove Keller in an almost obsessive manner; a desire that, in my opinion, finds such clear expression in almost no other writer and yet has lived and still does in more than one. I mean the dream of speaking as a writer from among the people, in their voice and without a name of your own that might separate and distinguish you from all the others; the dream of quite naturally saying the things that everyone else is thinking, feeling and wanting. Such that the difference between the writer—Keller, in our particular case—and the others would at most be that he'd be better at finding those common words. To have a name, for example Gottfried Keller, to speak as a delimited Gottfried Keller, to *have to* speak as such—when that happened to him, as was unavoidable, it wasn't a triumph for Keller but a defeat. The more famous he became, the greater was the failure of his original hope. Fame covered up a desire, while only ever half compensating for it, that had been much more radical than the banal wish to be admired as an individual. Likewise, fame told Keller he had not succeeded in—quite naturally—being at one with the feelings and thinking of people, generally. Had he really been, people wouldn't have cared about who had composed their songs and written their book. They'd simply have sung them like folk songs and read them as you would a book of folk tales.

Of course, such a dream isn't dreamt by all those who go on to achieve fame. Goethe was Prometheus from the word go and stole fire from the gods. Thomas Mann was never in any doubt that he knew better than his readers. Humility was not their thing. No, for them, fame was the necessary consequence of their uniqueness. Not for a moment did they become involved in the kind of conflicts in which Keller, so unsuspectingly and helplessly, got entangled. For the 'people'—and this is a platitude—are actually individuals, and they are stupid, loyal, shrewd, sharp as a tack, deceitful; sometimes also vain or kind-hearted; and at times, all these things at once. That the people represent the sum of many differences Keller knew too but deep within, he nurtured, nonetheless, the image of an oddly ideal equality of all. All good. All diligent. All with equal amounts of money. (Feeling exuberant, he was even, once or twice around 1848, to call himself a communist.) His desire to blend in would mean *too* that the terrible affronts to which he'd been exposed in the social milieu of his youth would cease to apply. That it was impossible to speak with everyone's voice, Keller first had to learn the painful way. Gradually and quite contrary to his original hopes, he at first became 'distinctive'. Almost against his will, he acquired 'distinctive' language — the utopian deviation from how the majority speak — and thus arrived at a 'name' for himself. Gottfried Keller.

The dream was over. Keller dreamt it more intensely than most — supported by his own private *and* public history — and, of course, he could only be disappointed. And that's what happened: he was greatly disappointed. His entire work, however much it might shine and sparkle, can also be read as the expression of a constantly growing disappointment. One that, at the end of his writing life, made him drop even poetry. Without poetry — this naive excess that meant both life and the possibility of happiness — he had no language at all any more. Old man Keller was wordless. In real terms, in his everyday life, he was mostly silent, and as a poet, now, always. First though, with *Martin Salander* — his splendid swansong, full of dissonance — he identified, in an incredible final feat, what had pushed its way in between him and the others: money, which from 1848 onwards had been 'working' more and more (that was how it was seen back then, also), and which led Keller to the sobering realization that democracy—even such ideally imagined democracy—was the most conducive form of state when it came to out-and-out moneymaking. Today, we are of the view that we, our generation, was the first to be exposed to a very new acceleration. But Keller's contemporaries had to learn in their day already how to hold on to the ever faster-turning wheel of history, if they didn't want to be hurled out into the universe somewhere. Those old days, when they were still the present, were anything but good. Exactly at the time of *Martin Salander*— as is also the theme of the book—money was beginning to go raving mad. Nowadays, it's trampling round the globe in such heavy-footed fashion, it's crushing whole swathes of land.

No wonder then that Keller's blend of poetry also fell victim to the new pressures—he could see this and bemoaned the fact but couldn't stop it—making way for a language that was arid. That was the price he paid for looking the Beast of Reality as fearlessly as possible in the eye. The gain was that his new sobriety enabled him no longer to take the blame for *everything*. How long his path to this point had been! With what rich means had he resisted! How much poetry he'd set against an unideal reality! In the end, however (as he now knew; the others couldn't understand what had made him so grumpy) he stood before the ruins of the dream that he'd never quite managed to let go. Okay, so he now had a name, a famous name — he was, to echo that old chestnut, world-famous in Zurich. But what he had to say was coming less and less from the centre, and more and more radically from the margins. He, the famous man, was now marginalized. When he died on 15 July 1891 the *Neue Zürcher Zeitung* appeared with a black border. On the front page, a single headline in bold print: *Gottfried Keller* and alongside it, the little cross that indicates death. The remainder of the page was filled with an obituary that revered him. Unwittingly, the minimalistic headline reflects the extent to which the life and work of Gottfried Keller had been reduced to only a name.

And yet, in the beginning, everything had been so full of hope. The times were favourably disposed to the dream of which we speak here. Others dreamt it too, other freedom singers like Georg Herwegh or Ferdinand Freiligrath, who, when the 1848 Revolution had begun to go wrong in their own country, fled to Zurich because from 1830 onwards, it had been the head and heart of the only state in Europe, in which democracy had asserted itself against authoritarian forms of government. Both Herwegh and Freiligrath were to treat Keller in friendly fashion. The incomparable Büchner had already come to Zurich in 1836 — 'wanted' posters had been put up for him back home — and I like to imagine the twenty-three-year-old Büchner and the sixteen-year-old

Keller running into each other in the lanes of the old town but without recognizing each other. (They lived less than two hundred metres apart.) Two very different people walked past each other on those occasions but at the heart of each was a very similar dream. That said, Büchner, by this point, had already abandoned the dream—he was more radical, sharper and had fewer illusions than Keller—and his early death meant that he couldn't dream to the end the dream of being at one with everyone in his particular way.

In *Der grüne Heinrich*, Keller describes his ideal: 'Wide-eyed, the crowd first contemplates the individual who wishes to say something to it,'—the writer, that is, Keller himself *was* one and was in the process of becoming *even more* of a writer with this book—

> and this individual, bearing up, courageously, reveals his best side in order to prevail. He shouldn't think, however, in terms of being their master; for others have been there before him, and others will come after him, and each was born of the crowd; he is a part of it, a part that the crowd confronts, wishing to conduct an uplifting conversation with itself in the form of him, its child and property. *Every true public speech is just a monologue that the people conduct with themselves.* Happy, though, is he who—in his own country— can be a mirror that reflects nothing but these people, with the people themselves being just a small bright mirror of the living world.[11]

Keller failed. And he suffered so much in the face of his failure that one would like to call out, to comfort him and tell him that failure has been the lot of *every* writer since the beginning of time. The first singer of all humanity, Orpheus, failed, failing the very task that, unchanged, has remained ours to this day: to conquer death with poetic song. We have all been failing ever since, and Samuel Beckett's pathetic-and-witty formula—that popped its head round the door in my first lecture already and that I shall now quote properly—has naturally become familiar to us: 'Try again. Fail again. Fail better.' [12]

Every writer is a roly-poly doll; has to be; and Keller was one who got a punch on the nose more often than average. Each time, he picked himself up and repositioned his mirrors that were intended to reflect the people. We have no reason to sneer at the apparent naivety of his dream. It was—after Orpheus' dream, of which Keller didn't ever lose sight either—the second greatest dream a writer can dream. It's a splendid dream that the twentieth century, however, has muzzled in the hearts and heads of its writers. Because an era in which millions of perpetrators killed millions of victims deprived that desire—the desire to be at one with everyone—of nourishment. And yet. Nowadays, too, the likes of us start off with hopes like that, even simply in the sense that our childhood years—if they pass in any way harmoniously—lead us to believe in the paradise of being at one with everything and everyone. We leave this paradise only reluctantly, even if it's a case of having no other choice when, finally, we understand death. This is the experience of all human beings, but writers are perhaps a little more recalcitrant. The dream of finding words for, and making sense of, what we have in common and of sharing a mutual understanding of these things can be found in any age, and, of course, also in the twenty-first century.

The years before 1848 were much more favourably disposed to such dreams. The moment of victory was able to confirm for Keller—indeed, *had to* confirm for him—that the dream had become reality. A childhood dream had been fulfilled, the lifelong dream also of his father, who died when Keller was five, on whose shoulders Keller stood all his life, whose political dreams he adopted and radicalized; and eventually brought to a successful conclusion. Happiness, as we know, is a childhood wish that has been fulfilled and if ever Keller—who always lived with his 'quiet underlying sorrow'—attained happiness, then it was in those moments when the private and the public became one for a brief moment in history.

Isn't it odd that this Gottfried Keller, who with a shotgun in hand had set off to fight the conservatives and the clerics, should not then wish in any way to enjoy the fruits of victory together with his (democratic) fellow citizens? Instead, he immediately absconded to Germany, initially to Heidelberg and then to Berlin, that is, to the very place that was the heart of the most authoritarian exercise of power. He literally *fled* to that Berlin from which many of his brothers and sisters were escaping to Switzerland in the opposite direction. They were now based in Zurich, not Berlin, with the result that my home town, for a few years, became a centre of the most exciting political and artistic progress. Gottfried Semper and Wilhelm Richard Wagner. High German became the everyday ordinary language of the local intellectuals too. But Keller was no longer part of that. What had driven him from Zurich so quickly? How did the man who had just written, with great excitement: 'No, private individuals can no longer exist!'[13] and 'Woe betide anyone who doesn't link his own fate to that of the public, for he will not only not find any peace but, in addition, lose his inner grip [. . .] He who is not for us, is against us. May he simply participate in order that the decision be accelerated,'[14] so soon after his cause had triumphed, abscond so quickly to a place where, certainly, no one was looking for him? He, who had just been shouting 'Ça ira!' and who saw his poetry as his 'lifeblood' that he had 'spat out', as the 'battle cry' that had to 'be boomed out'. 'For ours is the whole, beautiful world!' he had rejoiced, and 'Oh my homeland! Oh, my fatherland! How dearly, ardently, I love you' and 'Yoicks! Yoicks! The hounding starts! Big and small are coming riding!' and 'Bang bang! Boom bang boom!' and 'Meek, tricolour lass / Dress again, ready to dance / O Swiss glacier / Gleam in the morn anew!' and 'Raise your shield now, patron saints / of all peoples, for the fight!' or, finally, 'O May blossom, o freedom tree / So youthful and so green / How you'll bloom, that human dream, / and bloom and bloom forever!'[15]

Perhaps Keller fled from Switzerland in order not to have to write any more poems like these. In all the turmoil, he lost all sense of himself and needed a place to find himself again, or, rather, find himself for the first time. He needed distance, distance from the self-sure mood of victory among the progressives and, no doubt even more so, from his private circumstances. From his mother, first and foremost. He, who was forced by an odd fate to live in the same house as his mother until his forty-fifth year, no doubt, would have preferred to lay an ocean between him and her. The mother's death at the end of *Der grüne Heinrich* can, of course, also be read as wish-fulfilment. As a successful murder. Because *that* is why Heinrich had—seemingly pointlessly—hung round the riflemen's festival in Basel for three days: to make sure his mother, when he did return, was definitely dead. In literature, his plans worked out. In real life, while returning from Munich, Keller had idled the three days away in Frauenfeld. When he then, finally, did get home, his mother was happy as a lark and more ready than ever to stoke his feelings of guilt with words and deeds.

Viewed this way, what is astonishing is the fact he did not immediately immigrate to America and write *Der grüne Heinrich* somewhere in the Wild West. Whole villages sailed over the Atlantic back then to found 'New Sumiswald' or 'New Glarus'. But Keller did not found a 'New Hottingen'—nowadays a district close to the centre of Zurich, Hottingen was still an independent village in

1848. He chose Berlin, staying, at least, where his language was spoken. And so he could write *Der grüne Heinrich* and lend powerful expression to his pain. The escape from Zurich, straight away, in 1848, became the turning point in his life. He was now almost thirty, after all. If we are strict with him — and why shouldn't we be — he'd written nothing up till then that would draw us out from the woodwork, with the exception of two or three mysteriously splendid poems that read like cries for help from his inner darkness:

WINTER NIGHT

Every wing in the world had fallen.
The white snow lay still, glittering.
No cloud hung in the stars' pavilion.
No wave hammered the hard lake.

The lake's tree came up out of the depths
Till its top froze in the ice.
The lake spirit climbed up the branches
And looked hard through the green ice, upwards.

I stood on the thin glass there
That divided the black depths from me;
I saw, limb by limb, her beauty
Pressed close under my feet.

Through muffled sobbing her hands
Played over the hard lid.
I have not forgotten that lightless face;
It rises in my mind without end, without end.[16]

The poem was written just before 1848, a year or two earlier. And we might be permitted to think, indeed *must* conclude, that Keller himself is the lake spirit that can't break through the ice into freedom. Not yet. The ice broke or melted only in Berlin. Berlin was where the miracle of Keller finding himself happened, a miracle so great that he himself only partly noticed. He considered *Der grüne Heinrich* to be a failure. He, indeed, had an unusually strong talent for denigrating himself. It hurts again and again to see how this man, overflowing with talent, who tried to love the world and the people in it so intensely, felt himself to be a loser all his life. That's right: it wasn't an Icarus that took off from Zurich; not at that point, for sure. If ever one did flap his wings, he could immediately foresee his fall—and he approved of it, actually. Only in our times, I reckon, has that form of social control been on the wane—everyone on a level playing field, everyone focused on the same thing—the one that we puritan peasants or peasant puritans still, even today, from time to time regard as necessary in order to attain that greater malaise that, alone, allows us to permit ourselves to feel well. In Gottfried Keller, in any case—a freethinker guided by Ludwig Andreas von Feuerbach—the Zwinglian God was on the rampage all Keller's life, in the form of ineradicable feelings of guilt.

Only far away from his homeland did Keller then manage to duck away from these disastrous mechanisms and put structures in place against the pain swamping him. He now found that appropriate distance to pain—not so close as to be overwhelmed, not so far away as no longer to recognize it—which allowed him to look pain in the eye. Yes, indeed, the ice between him and the lake spirit may also be a symbol for that. Now, behind the ice—close, but a safe distance away—the pain became visible and comprehensible. All those things that, very recently, had been a hazy muddle and had swamped his heart and brain like lava, now became portrayable.

On his long way towards taking disappointment in his stride, he often stumbled, took one step forward, two back, then another three forward. He was anything but a patient sufferer. His private pains played cheap tricks on him—in his everyday life, in any case. Again and again they also distorted what he was writing. Often he could only 'solve' his problems by avoiding them in his writing. His terrible experiences with women, first and foremost. And so he probably leant on the crutch of irony more often than was good for his work. And if he'd found something beautiful— think: Judith, naked—he often took it back later. 'He was quite timid in reading his own works,' as Walter Benjamin put it.[17] And, one might add, at times also when *writing*. The strategy of *Der grüne Heinrich*, in which he traced the line of his childhood pain with the greatest of courage, unswerving consistency and a glowing heart, was no longer available to him in *The People of Seldwyla*, his next major book. He did not wish, or was not able, to subject himself right away to the same exertion again, and had not grasped—or only in part—that precisely in *Der grüne Heinrich*, he'd been closer to the people than ever before, to his ideal, exactly *because* he was able to say what the misery and the happiness of an individual were. Thus, the Seldwyla stories are often underlaid with satire, often marked by a somewhat tortured, humane irony and at times, they are touchingly unabashed dreams of atonement. The whole disappointment with life is hallucinated away in a radical fashion. The story, for example, which is known as 'Frau Regel Amrain' but is, above all, about her son, is an almost comically radical repair job on a bad reality. Everything turns out well in the story, everything that—in Keller's real life—went wrong. Above all, 'Frau Regel Amrain' is nothing less than a shamelessly open Oedipal fantasy. It is the story of the delightful little Fritz, whom his mother loves dearly and rears to manhood—there's no father anywhere to be seen—with her loving robustness and affectionate sense of humour. All the misery of Keller's childhood is revoked piece by piece. Like a bookkeeper, Keller ticks off point after point, rewriting the misfortune of the past as good fortune in the present. Point one: in real life, Keller's mother—when he was seven and his father had been dead for two years—married her husband's journeyman and was now called Frau Wild. In the story, a journeyman also tries to woo Frau Regel Amrain—very wildly, even—and he closes in on the goal of his desires so vigorously that Frau Amrain 'sighs deeply' and is about to 'allow herself what pleasure and refreshment had to offer'.[18] At that very moment, though, little Fritz, that is, a barely disguised little

Gottfried, turns up unexpectedly, and what's more — it couldn't be any clearer, really — he's carrying 'a long curtain rod with a thick gold-plated knob on the end'.[19] He scares off the wooing journeyman once and for all, so much so, that the latter — barely is he out the door, and has the full stop been placed at the end of the sentence — is never mentioned again, even briefly. He's gone, for ever. And Mama, though considerably aroused and somewhat dishevelled, isn't in any way angry with her son but infinitely grateful. From that moment onwards, she attends only to him, him, him. Then, point two: His father's death was probably the greatest shock in Keller's life. From one moment to the next, his father had vanished from his life. In the story, however, the father — thought to have gone forever — suddenly returns. Resurrected from the dead. That is huge, and the greatest possible good fortune. Although. Immediately, the *writing* Keller becomes aware of the risk of this most wondrous of all wish-fulfilments — that the father, suddenly alive again, could regain the place in his mother's affections that is now his — and so he straight away dims down the father's presence to that of an old man who limits himself to being grateful that his son is so diligent and is clearly making his wife so happy. For Fritz, young Keller's alter ego, is running the business — point three — competently and intelligently. He secures — point four — a delightful wife and has lovely children, thus also correcting Keller's misery with women. Point five: Fritz Amrain, as did once the young Keller, takes part in two franc-tireur processions. But Fritz is *not* persuaded to turn back by the police unlike Keller once was, already in Albisrieden, deplorably far from the aimed-for battlefield. Rather, *he* gets as far as the Central Switzerland of the evil Jesuits and bravely fires his shots, and unlike the real Keller, he *does* have caps in his gunlock. *He* learns his political lesson, which is, not to allow juvenile posturing to make one look ridiculous. And indeed, Keller even succeeds, at the end of the story, in transforming the mother's death—clearly, the mother has to die too—into a triumph. This time, no blame can be attached to the son. 'She herself, when she died, stretched out proudly, even in death, and never before was such a long woman's coffin carried into the church; and one that bore such a noble corpse to Seldwyla.'[20]

Only on one other occasion did Keller permit himself an even more obvious transformation of disappointment into longed-for happiness: in *The Banner of the Upright Seven* which, for a very long time now, has been his best-known and most popular piece of prose. It is set in the delicate spring of the young democracy in 1849 but it was written in 1860—when wishful thinking no longer helped. After only twelve years, everyday banalities had the upper hand again. Probably for that reason, too, the *Banner*—even more crassly than the earlier 'Frau Regel Amrain'—became a veritable orgy of wish-fulfilment. The story—with its need to have *everything* end well—seems somewhat greedy.

In *Banner*, the successful revolution belongs once more to those who created it. The liberalism of old—which no longer existed in Keller's present (just about)—is alive once more. Once again, an innocent people celebrate. But it is so innocent and *so* good that the story itself soon has the reader suspecting that Keller wants the reality of 1860 to be turned back—by the magic of words—into the ideal world of 1848. Keller has indeed abandoned his idea—genetically coded in him, as it were—of quite naturally being the voice of everyone while remaining nameless. He *had to* abandon it—and very soon, at that—after the experience of writing *Der grüne Heinrich*, which for him, for that very reason, became a rude awakening, and so—not least for that reason—he considered his novel to have failed. Heinrich, this culpable loser, was *unable* to embody the people as a whole.

The sobered-up Keller concluded:

And thus now, the beautiful mirror that was meant to reflect its people was shattered, and the individual who wanted to be part of the majority was broken. For having destroyed the immediate life source that linked him to his people, he no longer had the right, and the honour, to function alongside them. If you wish to improve the world, clean up outside your own front door first, as they say.[21]

It was to prove that Keller couldn't live with a completely shattered mirror. And so he put together a working concept for himself: a good Swiss compromise between the original ideal and the radical disappointment expressed at the end of *Der grüne Heinrich*.

'I consider it the duty of a poet,' as he was to explain his new theoretical crutch to his publisher Berthold Auerbach, 'not merely to glorify the past, but to strengthen the present, the germs of the future, and beautify it in such a manner that people may still be able to believe: yes, we are like that, and that is the course of our life.'[22] These thoughts are beautiful and noble, but in practice and truth, Keller couldn't—not yet—bear what *Der grüne Heinrich* had suggested to him: he was *not* speaking in the voice of the people but—quite the opposite—was at ever greater odds with commonly held views. In *Banner* he wished, at least for the duration of the story, to be allowed to bathe in his ideals again. And he ran a full bath, as if knowing it would be his last. He was never again to write so deliberately unbrokenly, 'positively', if you like. Because for whatever reasons he's regarded as one of the great realists of the nineteenth century, we occasionally forget that he became a realist very reluctantly. If at all, indeed, he was one. Keller was a magician but a conjurer whose magic—under the pressure of the real world—worked out less and less well, and who, finally, completely gave up.

A word now about that 'green', mentioned in the very title of his first book. The *Banner*, too, is a green story all the way through, even just for the fact that it is set at a national shooting match in Aarau—symbolically, in 1849— and shooting matches, back then, were a sea of green. For

green is the colour of that dream of which we speak here.
For Keller, it has just as strong associations as blue does for
Novalis. When a green turns up in Keller's work, we are
always close to the heart of his darkness and desire. There
is no casual green in Keller, and it always has both private —
intimate — and political connotations. His first, indeed, only
memory of his father is green. Little Gottfried is in the arms
of his father who is wearing a green coat and showing him
a — naturally, also green — potato plant, to explain to him
how, a few short years ago, it had saved little Gottfried and
his mama and papa from starvation. (There were two
famines in nineteenth-century Switzerland; the first around
1815, the second, less severe, in the years before 1848.) The
father's green coat, however — and that is the political part
of the story — was the uniform of his sharpshooters' club and
that indicated a reference to a radical political alignment.
Green was the colour of the imminent *coup d'état*. Keller, even
if he flirted for a few weeks with communism, was not a
Red. He was a Green.

Rather than on 'The Dream of Singing Anonymously
in the Voice of the People', I could have spoken today about
'The Disappearance of Colours from the Work of Gottfried
Keller'. I would have had to mention the same hopes and
disappointments. You can see at all times from Keller's
colours how he was doing. *Der grüne Heinrich* sparkles with
all the colours of the rainbow. Heinrich Lee walking through
the spring forest: your eyes blink, there is so much light. And
even the last, short chapter shines golden four times, blue

thrice, rosy twice, red and with a silver stripe once — and also black twice, for it does, after all, describe Heinrich Lee's funeral. The final sentence of *Der grüne Heinrich* is, of course, also green: 'It was a beautiful and pleasant summer's evening when they buried him with wonderment and sympathy, and on his grave there grew a very fresh and green grass.'[23]

In the final chapter of *Martin Salander*, there are then — as throughout the book — no colours any more. At one point, a snow-white cook, at another, a dark little pirate's boat. On the other hand, even on just the last page, you'll find 'goods', 'private property', 'envy', 'vanity' and 'document'. The new age has arrived. In it, a green Heinrich would be an absurdity from ancient times. And the green Gottfried had long since gone grey.

That's just about what I wanted to say to you today. I'll close with a word about our national team. Meanwhile, you see, the groups have been drawn for the 2010 World Cup in Novel Writing. Switzerland, ranked 43 internationally, was in pot 3, and we were immediately put in the same group as the USA, the favourite to win the tournament. Germany and Liechtenstein joined us. At the press conference that followed, the draw seemed to give our manager some cause for thought. 'It'll be bloody hard even just to get past the group stages,' he said. 'Take the Yanks: every single player, even the goalie, manages a thousand pages a year, easily. The Germans, too, have several heavyweights, and you can always count on Martin Walser, their centre forward, for a goal.' Peter von Matt, our national coach, added that he'd be dropping all those players from our squad who run out of steam after only a hundred and fifty or hundred and eighty pages. Me, then. And all the others too, actually. Peter Bichsel, Jörg Steiner, Gerhard Meier. Markus Werner. A pity. I'd have liked to play in another tournament with them and all the others. We'd been doing really well recently, too. And against Liechtenstein, we'd have had a real chance.

On Imagination, Megalomania,
Memory, Death and Life

Ladies and Gentlemen,

Today, I'd like to speak about imagination, megalomania, memory, death and life.

First, imagination. 'Power to the imagination' was
the call of many in those already mythical years around
1968 — although those for whom *power* was really what was
at stake despised imagination and perhaps feared it,
preferring to be guided by the rigid crash barriers of
ideology. Those who genuinely wished to introduce more
imagination into public life and also into their own were
no doubt less interested in power than in a fresh, more
free and more relaxed response to the existing — bad —
circumstances which, in this way, would have improved
somewhat. A little of the hoped-for greater public imagination was definitely achieved back then. Before 1968,
the world — at least that's what my memory tells me — was
more stubborn and greyer and — far more so than
nowadays — bolted down within borders that had been

drawn more in response to a dull insistence on bad traditions than to objective necessities.

Whatever. Imagination defies a definition, with which we would all immediately agree, without argument. It is so nimble, so mutable, diverse and good at taking us by surprise that we all know roughly what is meant by the term. But only with some effort and a degree of vagueness can we — as with time and the soul, too — begin to narrow the definition down. I, of course, immediately looked up what Freud says. He says, to put it very briefly, that fantasies are sexual desires — that our fantasies are triggered by the elemental force of urges — and writes about artists and fantasizing as follows: 'Apparently their constitutions' — those of artists — 'are strongly endowed with an ability to sublimize and to shift the suppression determining their conflicts [. . .]. The artist understands how to elaborate his daydreams so that they lose their essentially personal element, which would repel strangers and yield satisfaction to others as well.' A side remark from me: The artist's fantasy (or to stick to our subject: the writer's) does indeed only begin to be universal if readers pick up on this fantasy and — by reading — bring it to life within themselves. In contrast, for those who are not artists, Freud continues, 'The ability to obtain satisfaction from imaginative sources is very restricted. Their relentless suppressions force them to be satisfied with the sparse daydreams which may become conscious.'[24]

It has been and still is said of me that I have a lot of imagination. For many years, however, I wasn't aware that

I could have more imagination, or a different kind, than other people. I thought that since I was the way I was, others would be too. I didn't notice my imagination in any way and nor do I find any idealization of imagination in me. I try, on the contrary, to transfer the images of my at-times-seething fantasies into the bright light of reason. Nothing, in any case, ever comes out of you that didn't go in, at some point. There are people who are capable of going round the world in eighty days and when they return they have nothing to tell you as they think they haven't experienced anything. Anyone who doesn't see anything has nothing in his brain. But fantasies, even the most bewildering ones, are made out of reality. No one fantasizes about something that has its origins in a very differently defined unknown. In divine inspiration. Or a fourth, or one hundredth, dimension. Leonardo, too, extrapolated and interlinked familiar things, thus pushing towards the unknown; probably also Einstein, whose thoughts I am not capable of following. Delirium, too, has its roots in earthly things. Perhaps — as Klaus Hoffer put it — imagination is a suggestion that surprises also you yourself, and which comes from an interpretation of the world different from the one that is commercially available. Sometimes, I think imagination is nothing other than an especially good memory. In its dark attic — which, in my private working hypothesis, is devilishly similar to Freud's unconscious — memory stores everything it has ever seen, heard, smelled; really everything — that leaf, falling from the tree, which was immediately also dropped by your active memory, and the short sob of that woman, intercut on the news, mourning her child killed by a bomb, who—in your active memory—as a consequence of other monstrosities, is immediately deleted again. Suddenly, though—only the devil knows why—the falling leaf turns up again in a conscious fantasy, maybe decades later. That silent cry.— My scepticism or, let's say, controlled caution vis-à-vis the imagination—power to the imagination: anything but that!—has, indeed, to do with the fact that the imagination can be not only bright and enriching but also dark and menacing. It interconnects the inexhaustible material of what you have experienced; that is, terrible material too. Literature, it is true, is more often made from dark rather than bright fantasies.

'All supreme productivity,' said the old Goethe—who liked talking about the supreme, and whom I like to quote when I'd like to, too, but don't quite dare to do so in my own name—'stands not in anyone's power and is above earthly force. Man must regard these things as gifts from on high [. . .] and he must receive and venerate them with joyful gratitude. It is related to the daemonic which can overpower him and do with him as it pleases, and to which he gives himself up unconsciously, while believing himself to be acting under his own power.'[25]

Others have this experience too: when they are writing, they become a kind of filter for the words that are then on the page, and that they, the first readers, acknowledge almost as something alien. Who has written these words?

'It' has written them — I use the word loosely — and like a medium, you look at your fingers, what they are up to on the keys of the typewriter. A part of you that is barely visible to you is writing. The imagination has been detached from conscious planning and structuring; and part of the creative ability of a writer is surely being able to make space in his head — immediately, without fear and without using scissors — for the unexpected thing that turns up so abruptly, as much space as the surprise guest needs, simply, and being able to do this without losing all sense of direction. A creative achievement *without* imagination doesn't exist. $E=mc^2$, Einstein's most famous equation — which I, as I said, don't understand — is without doubt a tremendous achievement of his *imagination*. I shall say nothing of the rest, of the industry and craftsmanship of the highest level. In *Hamlet*, too, there is a lot of craftsmanship, of course, but imagination is *always* the source of literature.

'It' writes then — the imagination is in power — but 'it' writes more than 'ideas'. Never confuse 'an idea' with a productive suggestion from your imagination. Ideas come to all of us every sixty seconds and they are the death of all poetry. Anyone who has 'an idea' should throw it away as far as possible before he gets wound up in it, or the idea in him. 'It' — the form of imagination that is frequently very independent when it comes to the conscious — often moves in a mined area, such that — to the detriment of the text — we are repeatedly tempted to slam shut the door that for a moment appeared to be open. But 'it' not only knows about content—about that leaf floating down from the tree *and* the monstrosities from that dangerous and forbidden zone; 'it' also knows about form, about structure, about how a text breathes. Whether it should be in major or minor. Adagio or presto. 'It' knows better than you, better than your conscious craftsman's brain. When writing, perhaps the most difficult thing, and the least steerable, is the pace of a text, its density—every reader needs, here and there, *empty* sentences (as it were) that let him stop to breathe—feeling the weight of a particular part in connection with the whole, and this even more so since while writing, you have to keep an eye on two completely different speeds, the one that you, in real terms, *hic et nunc*, need for a passage of the text, and the pace that this passage then has within the whole. With the result that you can work for three days on half a page that, when read, scurries past like a cold gust of wind. You must never lose track of the pace of the text, however laborious the work on a particular part might be. This monitoring feeling—which dictates the changes in tempo and keys to you—knows more than you, you must rely on its suggestions—fed from its fundus of imagination—being right. Yes, writing, it's true, happens quickly but it can take a while before the text is in its final form and the details have found their right place within the bigger picture. Phew! Maybe that's why I'm someone who'll re-type a whole page if I make a typo in the bottom right-hand corner because, then, the imagination is faced with a sense of order that can sometimes take on compulsively exact features.

Why do, at certain times, imaginations that differ but point in the same direction virtually explode—we then call this the Renaissance or the Enlightenment or Romanticism—as if, like seeds, they had already been planted in the humus of time and had now all been watered at the same time by the same epoch-making rain? At different times, after years of unconscious—and, therefore, also unnoticed—incubation, and in different places similarly shaped fantasies can suddenly find expression. That the earth is round, that social being determines consciousness, that man is driven by sexual desire. Individuals who are not, actually, so completely isolated but do very much find an echo, then get—to use Alfred Lorenzer's phrase—to speak for the collective. And so the thought soon rears its head— it is thought by many—that the fantasies formulated by the great individuals would have found expression anyway, even if a brick had fallen on the head of the person who spoke for the collective before he could open his mouth or dip his quill in the inkwell. Five or six smaller minds would then have leapt into the gap and would have helped to work out those fantasies due in that epoch, because they were simply in the air and *had* to be formulated. I believe also that, at some point, someone *had* to write a *Ulysses*, even a *Finnegans Wake*. I am grateful to Joyce for sparing me the bother.

Nevertheless. The thought that writers express what everyone else is feeling but just can't say, is so fetchingly democratic, so wondrously humble—disburdening for the writer too, in the sense that (there being no awkward differences) he need no longer grate against the people round him—that it's perhaps too nice to be true. What if it were the other way round? If the best examples of literature, in contrast, were to express what only this one writer can see, and that without him would remain unwritten and unimaginable? What if a *single* poetic thought by one individual, emanating from his own creative imagination, could shape an entire age? Were it not to be formulated—because of that falling brick, for instance—would his era take a completely different turn?

At such heights of the imagination—imaginations of the century, so to speak—even the best only move in their finest hours. Genius doesn't happen every day, either. What is important is to recognize the minute in which the star begins to shine and, if possible, to make an hour of it. Because I do tend, as it happens, to the view that there is *no* substitute for a unique creative achievement. Perhaps even for the artist himself, there is no other time if he squanders the first time. Of course, this is the famously stupid question—'what would have happened if'—that is impossible to answer because Cleopatra just *did* have a beautiful nose and so Caesar went to bed with her immediately; and because the little Goethe who, as he reports in *Truth and Poetry*, 'through the unskilfulness of the midwife, came into the world as dead',[26] wasn't, it turned out, totally dead. Would someone else really have written 'Welcome and Farewell', and *Faust*? Shakespeare, at the first rehearsal of *Titus Andronicus*, falls from the stage and breaks his neck — no one would have written *Macbeth* in his place. No Mozart, no *Don Giovanni*. The imagination of the individual — even if he might one day speak absolutely for the collective — is unique. What hasn't been put into words remains unheard and, at most, a phantom pain indicates occasionally, in revenge, that we are lacking something, here and there. Perhaps, we living writers are those who try to fill — with what is missing — the void left behind by greater colleagues who came to an end too soon?

Second, megalomania. It is an often unrestrained part of our imagination and it doesn't have an especially good reputation. Even if we refer to it, more neutrally, as delusions of grandeur, it scores badly on our ethical rating scale. And yet, in the literature of all times books are teeming with delusions of grandeur, and the real lives of the writers — I am not speaking about dentists, lawyers or politicians here — are also, more than just often, determined by secret, or very publicly displayed, hopes of grandeur. I won't name names. Just imagine, for the sake of simplicity, the entire contents of the *Dictionary of World Literature*.

It's not unknown, for example, for me to imagine — a game of course; I had the idea at some point, at least — that a god is unrolling all of reality only for me. For me. Not for the others. The world is being made for me. To be more exact, it's constantly being produced in keeping with my needs. A game, remember, a game! I go that way, this way, and the god, at his switch point, quick as a flash, puts down a new road, puts out people who are bustling about, all only for as long as I pay them any attention. Behind me, the god rolls the landscape up again—I don't need it any more, after all, nor does he. Sometimes, when I am erratic and scoot now this way and then that, possibly even on my motor scooter, the god doesn't half have to get a move on. But, other days, I just have a doze or even sleep hour after hour. The god can then relax a little too, and—with a casual wink—keep an eye on me, just.—You're laughing. But other people's narcissistic fantasies that exclude one can also trigger a sense of discomfort. No doubt, you feel it too. The reason for the discomfort is: we cannot bear it if someone sees everything only in terms of himself, even the things most detached from him, and perceives us and the rest of the world, if at all, only in his projection that distorts almost everything.

I know another version of the fantasy I've just told you about, incidentally, in which the whole staging of reality is a manoeuvre of massive proportions, designed to deceive you, as part of which all the other people—or the afore-mentioned, by-now-malicious god—put a world down in front of you, the beauty and splendour of which, or, alternatively, its sober actuality, is a mere sham, an optical illusion that is being projected before you. Behind this Potemkin flickering is real life; things are as they really are. Everyone can see it, everyone knows it, except you. Maybe, the horizon—those blue mountains there, the sky—is merely painted, and if you were to go there, you could kick your way through the screen and *see*. Finally. You'd see a horror, presumably, but you'd no longer be the dupe.

All too often, delusions of grandeur are what future writers—and, no doubt, many others—use to pull themselves out of the bog of their circumstances, like Baron von Münchhausen, whose adventures, time and again, are delusions of grandeur that, unlike many of the more adult power fantasies of other writers, end positively. Yes, delusions of grandeur need not in any way necessarily and always lead us into the misery of hubris from which we'll never find our way out again, they help us just as often to bear our first steps in life. Even children, actually all children, help themselves with often richly elaborate hallucinations regarding their own power and significance. I—while the bullets of parental conflicts were zinging round me—could stand, invulnerable, in the middle of the crossfire and register absolutely none of it, because in my own head I was, for example, a bus driver for the Schweizer Alpenpost and steering my Saurer up round the bends of the Bernina Pass, that is, its realistic equivalent inside my skull. At some point, I had reached the top of the pass and—unnoticed by me—my mother and father had long since made up. Rather, my father had slammed the door behind him and my mother had gone, sniffling, into the kitchen.

It's said that adults, too, are capable of remaining completely absorbed. Scientists and artists, in particular. Dante, the story goes, was once reading a book that he couldn't take home, at a pharmacy in Siena, and he was reading so avidly, he didn't notice at all the tournament taking place outside on the Piazza del Campo, involving a few dozen whinnying horses, all thundering past. Engrossed in thought, Balzac would march off in the middle of the night, in his nightshirt and slippers, and discover to his surprise the next morning that he was on the Place de la Concorde. Hölderlin went to Bordeaux on foot and by stagecoach and, upon arriving, didn't recall the journey. He'd been thinking about other things. And in Egypt, Flaubert failed to observe the cataracts of the Nile — he'd taken the long boat trip to see them — because he'd been lost in thought, brooding about something. On the way back, he suddenly jumped up, shouting, 'J'ai trouvé. Eurêka. Eurêka. Je l'appellerai Emma Bovary. Bovary!'[27] I've got it! Eureka. Eureka. I'll call her Emma Bovary. Bovary!

Goethe, who asked *all* the questions that could be asked at that time and who also answered them all, if not always correctly, also has an answer for the delusions of grandeur of children. Or rather, he tells a story in *Truth and Poetry* that he thought up as a boy, in which he, little Johann Wolfgang, rescues three ladies from the powers of evil. In keeping with all the rules of power fantasies is the moment when the evil leader, a powerful magician, has to acknowledge he's up against someone bigger and more powerful, that is, Johann Wolfgang.

> 'Who then are you,' he asked in defiance, 'who dares speak thus?' 'A favourite of the gods,' I said, 'on whom it depends whether these ladies shall find worthy husbands and pass a happy life.' [. . .] The

old man cast himself down before me, without shrinking from the wet and miry soil; then he arose without being wetted, and took me kindly by the hand.'

'Now it may well be conceived,' Goethe then says, 'how often I repeated to myself this story, which I could hardly believe.'[28] Like the majority of us, Goethe, who had a fount of more stories with a similar pattern, later refrained from such unbridled wish-fulfilment fantasies. Like most writers, he found it much more difficult than most other people. What is *Faust*, if not a power fantasy, albeit one beset with the brunt of the real? And Goethe is, of course, not the first and only person to respond like this. Gilgamesh. And Icarus flies towards the sun — *the* dream of grandeur to top all others — and there are certainly also versions of the story in which the realistic morale of the father doesn't prevail and the feathers don't melt. Icarus disappears into the sun, *is* the sun, shines powerfully until the Day of Judgement. — Not in every case of someone who then grows up are the childlike rescue fantasies so well preserved as in the case of Karl May, whose inventions did indeed rescue him, in psychological *and* in economic terms, and who, when as an old man he travelled the Orient, the setting of many of his books, nonetheless broke down as no one there recognized him. Kara Ben Nemsi. Karl, the son of the Germans. — And what are the stories of *One Thousand and One Nights*, if not an almost never-ending sequence of fantasies in which one, or many, of those who speak for the collective fulfil absurdly unreal yearnings for richness and power? Yes, some guy or other occasionally scores with a princess but what matters in these fantasies — famous precisely for their sensuality — is much less erotic fulfilment and more money, power and glamour.

Children, who always imagine their rescue ideas more carefully and more vigorously, not only rescue themselves from a pressing situation but also shape their first adventures in their heads, writing *avant la lettre*, often more tightly and more wildly than they'll ever dare to again. These childhood fantasies transition seamlessly into the written word. The interface is the moment in which the child, the grown child, takes a pen and records in words what he fantasized. No work by any writer materializes out of thin air, from a bold, rational decision. On the contrary, the lead-up to it is long, *lifelong* so to speak. What, for many people, remain fantasies that were shut off or pushed into oblivion out of shame — fantasies in which the first-person hero was the best, the most beautiful, the strongest and cleverest — are made public in the case of writers. Shame, which in literature too gets in the way of confessions, is suspended, something which, in the case of thoughts of grandeur, whose deceitful companions are envy and grievance, is much more difficult than, say, with erotic confessions. Our intimate behaviour causes no shame; it should simply remain intimate. There are much more weighty reasons for shame than those relating to sexuality. Betrayal. A lie. Or simply the fact that we thought we were just great, and then someone else was able to do what we do ten times more precisely and a hundred times more gracefully. Or, even worse, the thing we got so excited about was dull and banal. An injustice even, a crime. These things cause shame to overflow. — We learn to understand that, yes, we can ask life questions, but that life gives us answers that aren't the ones we hoped for. Only now, when life is beginning to pile on serious pressure, do we learn to accept Beckett's sentence about always failing better. To lose the game of life with the greatest acquiescence available to humanity requires a proper dose of humility and insight.

Third, memory. In the beginning, and then for many years, we never doubt for a second we have one. Later, we know it's still more or less in working order so long as we can still remember the name of the illness that's stealing it from us. Sontheimer, or something. 'Memory is the only paradise,' Jean Paul says, 'from which we cannot be driven,'[29] and he says it either with bitter irony or with a barely believable naivety. Of course, we can be driven from the paradise of memory — and what's more, it isn't a paradise. We writers like to say of ourselves: we storytellers are like elephants when it comes to memory, because — simply — imagination is another word for memory and because everything that comes out of us has, indeed, at some point gone in. 'Once upon a time', this ingenious first line of the Brothers Grimm could actually be the opening sentence of *all* narrative literature.

Perhaps we storyteller-writers do have especially good memory. It may be the case but needn't necessarily be.

Quite possibly, we remember things at times less fearfully
and perhaps also in a more ordered way. More sensuously
and in more exact detail. It's no doubt a strength of writer-
storytellers that, whenever they want, they can conjure up
within, every period of their life. The age of eight. Twenty-
eight. Sixty-eight. In such a way that what's remembered
then *lives* and is linked with the now. Isn't split off and
enclosed in a glass coffin. I do, indeed, see the past — not
only my past but also history — within me as a continuous
stretch of way, a road heading towards the horizon with
many bends that, I don't know why, have impressed
themselves upon me, and that, whenever this visualization
of the past befalls me, always run the same way. From today
until about 1945, the path is halfway straight, rising slightly
beneath a bright sun, heading towards the rear. Then it turns
to the left and runs beneath a much more artificial light and
parallel to the horizon until, let's say, 1930, and then runs
parallel to the left edge of the picture, so to speak, back
towards me again, although farther away, smaller now and
in a light that is poorer still. So the First World War is on
the left there, still quite visible. Then the path fades, turning
left again — yes, it's trying to become a spiral, an eternally
spiralling loop — and disappears into the night of the
nineteenth century.

Whenever we writers invoke our memories, don't
forget that we are responsible for the material. And it's only
logical that we should narrate what we remember and not
what has been lost. The blind nucleus isn't selected as

material and the reader has to deduce it from the subtext. Nonetheless, I reckon that even nowadays—when so many different media can offer to perform the function of memory—literature is richest when it comes to laying down the memory of that period in time which, at the time of composition, is the present, and which has then passed so suddenly that future generations would have only a jumble of statistics and journalistic reports at their disposal, if our stories didn't exist. What would we know about Russia at the time of the Napoleonic Wars without Tolstoy's *War and Peace*? About life in the French provinces, in the late nineteenth century, without Flaubert? And about the life of peasants in Switzerland without Gotthelf, whose real name was Bitzius, and who was an archconservative vicar and capable, in his imagination—that is, in *The Black Spider*—of killing off every man and everything in the Emmen Valley where he lived? Everyone dead. Except him.—In the best cases, also those books we write without this goal in mind will come to express *our* epoch and preserve it more sensuously than documents could ever do. Just as, with old films, another splendid form of memory, we often respond more rapturously to the unintended messages than to those that were intended, that is, to the clothes, the hairstyles, the cars, the shop signs and the hats.

How many books have I read? Hundreds. Two or three thousand, for sure. More, probably. It all mounts up over the years. Whole libraries have left behind nothing more than a white flickering in the conscious part of my brain.

In the case of those to which my brain gives preferential treatment and doesn't simply let sink into oblivion, I remember, at least, a special climate, a tone that only this book has, a very special colour of memory. I thought I would demonstrate for you here, in real time, so to speak, how much—or, rather, how little—I still know about a book, and not just any average tome, but a work of major importance in world literature. Proust's *Remembrance*, because it's so wonderful, of course, because its very title requires this kind of task, *In Search of Lost Time*, and because it's been a long time since I read it. I didn't want to cheat or test myself in public. It's not possible: memory is a tad too detailed to be played out, step by step, before you. Nonetheless. The result is staggering. I can still reasonably remember the beginning, the way to the castle, the light, the hawthorn, Mama and her goodnight kiss, and later, the young women on the beach at Balbec. Is that the name of the place, Balbec? The coquettish lover, more than anyone else. And then a few very isolated scenes, through to the homosexual baron, whose name I've also forgotten— Malthus? Bothus?—and who does something with the groom in the stable, and the readers, I think, had to guess while reading what it was, rather than being told outright. Yes, I can remember clearest of all what wasn't described.—My wife, by the way, was able to remember right away what the baron's name was: Charlus.

As you can see, this is a proper coming out. I am doing it in the—no doubt—vain hope of finding a supportive community: men and women courageous enough, like at Alcoholics Anonymous, to step out before the group and admit that yes, I too, I too once read the *Elective Affinities* and can hardly remember a word of it. I too, I too devoured *Don Quixote* and can just about remember Rocinante, Sancho Panza and the windmills—because they've become part of folklore. At my age, among retired academics, one doesn't read any more anyway, one rereads. 'I have just reread *Medea*,' even if it was their first time.

At the same time, how many splendid books there are that I haven't read! All of Turgenev. All of Dickens, with the exception of *David Copperfield*. Every single philosopher, so to speak. Stifter's *Witiko*. And in the case of *The Man Without Qualities*, I've never got past the meteorological beginning. It is, indeed, distressing. Conversely, isn't it splendid that there are more masterpieces than we can ever read? Only crime fiction—in that case, there's clearly too little that is good. If ever that terrible illness—the name of which I can still remember, Alzheimer's—catches up with me, a library containing a *single* masterpiece will suffice either way. *Moby Dick*, for example. I'd read it again and again, once, ten times, and the eleventh time I'd close the book after the final sentence that I had read as if for the first time, and I'd leave this world and forget *everything*.

I'm planning, by the way, *not* to read again those books I've forgotten everything about, bar the title. I'll write them myself, the next time. It seems easier to me, somehow, to reinvent the work of Thomas Mann rather than read it from beginning to end. *Buddenbrooks* would be a short novella about two brothers, James and John Buddenbrook, who run a dodgy bookie's in London. Horse-racing bets, etc. *A Man and His Dog* would tell of the tender relationship between a gentle private scholar and his Rottweiler that, in the end, *does* eat him alive. And on the Magic Mountain would live the last magicians of our age; powerless now and, incapable of anything else, they'd put spells on one another, give one another pimples on the nose, for instance. — Or the *oeuvre* of Henry Miller! Read many decades ago very enthusiastically and now forgotten. But what amazing titles, to which I could add the content they deserve! *Tropic of Cancer* would tell the moving story of a young woman who would get cancer and, in the end, recover after all. *Big Sur* would be about Big Sur, a two-metre-tall Indian from the Navajo tribe, whose peaceableness would take him as far as the White House, into which, however, he'd refuse to move, preferring to remain in his tepee, from which with the help of Manitou he'd end all the wars of the world. And in the *Colossus of Maroussi*, the Maroussi would be a bloodthirsty indigenous tribe on the Easter Islands and would eat the author just as he was about to finish his book, with the result that the book would break off mid-sentence. And thus, so would Miller's *oeuvre*.

That's how it goes. I promised at the beginning to talk to you about imagination, megalomania, memory, death and life. In that order. Now it's death's turn, I realize my time has almost ended. My unconscious has managed once again to avoid death, for — of course — death is, really, what literature is about. For as long as literature has been created, it has been screaming, in horror, at death. It has been mocking death, hiding from it behind harmless little things and jokes or marching up to it in imperious fashion. No writer has ever won his match against death, not even Canetti who went a long way in terms of keeping death at bay. The writer never forgets that death is waiting behind his back, infinitely calm and yet capable, with a sudden sway of the scythe, of ending the game there and then. How many books and plays also end, in story terms, with the death of their heroes! Anna Karenina. Werther. Hamlet doesn't survive his play, either. Indeed, we really resent a work of literature if its heroes remain alive, for the life of every human being ends only with that person's death; and besides, the heroes in the books are standing in for us, they die in our place, and so we, the readers, can escape once more, unlike Effi Briest or Kafka's hunger artist. Reading tragedies is soothing for that reason too: because *we* survive.

A literary text is always ambivalent. Everything also contains its opposite. When literature contemplates death intensely, life is meant just as much. With death breathing down its neck, it tests whether and to what extent we are still alive. Again and again, it makes us — we, who like so much to get caught up in the pettinesses of a petty life — aware of the pathos of life. It celebrates life passionately and with all its heart, precisely because life is so fragile and fleeting. We're not dead yet! All of us here — we're the latest to participate in the series of tests, carried out over millions of years, to see if maybe, just for once, a woman or man could be the first person *not* to die. Never to die. Someone has to manage it one day, to be the first to do so; so why not us? We only have to ensure we don't suffer the same fate as the man who was promised immortality by the gods, only to forget to ask for eternal youth. He's now about three thousand years old and lives near Thessaloniki. A handful of dried-out skin. Bones. Entrails. He doesn't even smell any more. And, if you visit him, it's hard to decide whether he's still enjoying life.

You are right. He's probably—more likely—a legend. A story. In real life, death triumphs. But in literature, life does.

On Oedipus the King *and Sophocles*

Ladies and Gentlemen,

Last time, I focused on the basics of poetry, on its origins, so to speak, and talked about life and death, and said this and that about the rest. Such an excursion into the general is always dangerous: how easy it is to crash and, with a lot of bluster, to preach to the converted. For that reason, I'd like, in my final lecture, to hold on to something concrete again. With the annual conference of the German Psychoanalytical Society approaching, I've been focusing on Oedipus, on *Oedipus the King* by Sophocles. I like the gentle pressure that such an enquiry exerts, just as I enjoy giving these lectures because they force me to think a little more precisely about the vague thoughts I have. So I've tried to do nothing other than read *Oedipus the King*, and then *Oedipus at Colonus*. 'Reread', as I'm sure you appreciate. I'd like to present the results of my reading to you now, even if, to add insult to injury, these were already published in *Akzente*.[30] Nevertheless, I shall risk one or two of you occasionally vaguely remembering something whenever I say something that, in this form, or a similar one, has already been published. I began my lectures in the here and now, and would therefore like to close them with a story that is well over two thousand years old and is still as alive as it was on day one.

For there are a few stories that have been told for ever and—hardly altered at all—have been passed on through the millennia because something about them—something beyond all trends—gets to people so powerfully, they cannot get them out of their heads, and so the stories *have to* be told, over and over. These stories are called myths, they are something approximating cultural fossils, whose roots are not known, even if it can be assumed that they represent memory traces of something that happened—not in this way, of course, but not completely differently either—in a concrete place at a concrete point in time. The story of Oedipus is one of the most tenacious and most powerful myths in human history, the origin of which is supposed by some to be in roughly 1100 BCE. (But already in the Old Babylonian epic about the creation of the world, Enuma Elish, which is, certainly, another five hundred years older again, the heroine has a leman who is her son.) The ur-Oedipus, in any case, goes back to times in which the writing of history is also mythical, even if there are many signs that people's lives together followed different laws and norms than in classical Athens around 430 BCE, which is when the most famous re-narration was written, that is, by Sophocles. Sophocles gave it a form that is so staggeringly coherent that, even today, it appears to be *the* most mythical of myths, though he very clearly had the militant, crisis-shaken, male-dominated present of Athens in mind when writing. Old elements like the Sphinx, or the very fierce rejection of the oracle at Delphi by Jocasta—in Sophocles' present, Delphi was the undisputed sanctuary of Apollo—remain in the story like old milestones.

This story was then passed on, down through the millennia, and withstood two-and-a-half thousand years, almost unscathed. Innumerable variations on the theme since. Seneca, Boccaccio, Hans Sachs, Pierre Corneille. Hölderlin's great translation. In the nineteenth century, there was less interest, it is true—August von Platen's *Der romantische Oedipus*, a literary satire, was long considered the ultimate—but in the twentieth century there was a powerful revival. Every second writer, if I might exaggerate, wrote his version of *Oedipus*. Hugo von Hofmannsthal, Jean Cocteau, André Gide, T. S. Eliot, Igor Stravinsky.—I don't wish to speak about Freud, who has a lot to do, of course, with the revival of Oedipus in literature. What he took from the story of Oedipus should not concern us here, in a lecture on poetics. I might just perhaps say, provisionally and superficially, that Sophocles was after a very different story from the one that then so fascinated Freud. No wonder, and perfectly legitimately, the latter took from the story precisely those elements that were of use to him and pushed the others aside.

Oedipus, then. We know the story. Yes, but we know it, as a rule, not so very exactly. We *all* know that Oedipus kills his father and sleeps with his mother. That's embedded deep within us. That seems to be the burning message of the story. And then we probably also remember the Sphinx, the gigantic winged girl that eats all the young men (no young ladies) who cannot solve her riddle. Perhaps we even recall the riddle itself: What goes on four legs in the morning, on two legs at noon and on three legs in the evening? Man, of course. What else? (The real puzzle about this riddle, seen from the viewpoint of today, is that the answer's so obvious. So why did hundreds of young Theban males fail to see it? One answer is, of course, that it is easier to answer such a question from a comfy seat in a heated room than when the maw of some monster as high as a mountain, is snarling above you. Oedipus was not only the cleverest of the bold, young men — he was that, too; the play stresses right at the outset his godlike intelligence — he was also, above all, the coolest. And the Sphinx — that is, Sophocles — also knew that the most difficult thing is to recognize oneself. 'Here I am myself!' Here, at the beginning, Oedipus easily identifies what he was later to find so incredibly difficult to see. — And yes, Oedipus has injured feet, swollen feet — we recall that too; and, of course, that it all ends badly.

When and where does the story actually begin? With Oedipus' birth, or perhaps generations before that already

—he would then be merely the latest in a much longer string and would have to lie in the bed his forefathers had made for him—with Cadmus perhaps, the founder of Thebes (the brother of Europa, incidentally) who was the first—a recurring theme in this family—to get into conflict with the gods? They all quarrelled with different gods and goddesses. With Apollo, first and foremost. The great-grandfather, the grandfather, the father. With the last named Laius, Apollo then finally had had his fill and condemned the ruling dynasty to extinction. (Laius, by the way, was himself an adopted child—just as Oedipus was to become one—and seduced his stepbrother.) Laius learnt from the oracle at Delphi, the wording was in no way opaque, that if he fathered a son, the latter would kill him. (Daughters didn't have particularly great status at the time. *No longer had*, one can probably also say.) He dismissed the threat and impregnated Jocasta, out of greed and megalomania, and because he wasn't sober that night. Jocasta was also beautiful and had barely turned thirteen or fourteen. A boy was born and wasn't given a name, or the name hasn't survived, in any case, for the name by which the world knows him, Oedipus, means swollen foot, and he had these swollen feet because the nameless two-day-old had his feet bound together so tightly that no blood could get into them. —The royals had been arrogant enough to father a child but then simply to kill it, in the bedroom or the backyard, went against their sensitivities. A shepherd had to abandon it on Mount Cithaeron for the wolves to eat. The royal parents thought they could have their cake and eat it: the future murderer of Laius would be rendered harmless and they would remain innocent of the child's homicide. (Abandoning children, incidentally, was a widespread form of birth control, and didn't have the absolutely terrible associations that we feel nowadays. Why his feet were mutilated is something we can only speculate about. My favourite hypothesis is that the ghost of the dead child would thus be unable to haunt the dreams of his guilty parents.)

The shepherd climbed—hesitating to commit the terrible act—up the mountain and when he was right at the top and, on the other side, could see far out to the sea and down onto Corinth in the distance, he ran into a fellow shepherd with his herd. 'The gods have sent you!' And he placed the infant in the man's arms so quickly, the latter only realized what was happening when the shepherd was already running towards the first olive trees, far below. The second shepherd was a servant of the king and queen of Corinth, who were not blessed with children of their own. We need also to imagine royal dynasties of the time such that the king and queen, when they crossed their estates, were very much known to exchange a few words occasionally with their carriage makers, swineherds or shepherds. No wonder then that, that same evening, they were already holding the shepherd's little present in their arms. They adopted it. 'Never shall we tell him his wretched origin,' they swore to each other. 'Never.'—The child now had a name. Swollenfoot. Many said it to mock him. Soon, though, it was the name of the king's son.

Everything went well, for everyone, for many long years. In Thebes, Laius and Jocasta ruled in contented chastity over a flourishing town. In Corinth, Polybius and Merope were delighted with their son—he was growing up, his voice would soon break—and ruled the town with a mild severity. The sun shone down on all of them. No wars. No plague. Good harvests. Good rain showers, autumn after autumn. Celebrations. Hospitality.

Soon Oedipus was old enough to have a glass of wine with the others, or three glasses, and at his very first banquet, he ran into a courtier who had been at the court for decades and was already a bit tipsy, pissed as a newt, to tell the truth. Your man put an arm round his shoulders and slurred, 'I need to tell you something funny, Oedi. Your parents aren't your parents at all. You are a swollenfoot, I mean, you have two swollen feet. Have you never thought anything of it?' Oedipus became sober there and then and went home, on feet that were hurting him like they'd not done for years.

What the drunk had said he could not get out of his head. He summoned up all his courage and asked his father and his mother, and their faces turned pale and red, and the father roared, how dare he find out, this courtier, he'd read him the Riot Act like the Riot Act had never been read to anyone for as long as anyone could remember. The mother had tears in her eyes and took Oedipus tenderly into her arms. He calmed down a little, but not much. Then without telling anyone, he set out on his way to the oracle at Delphi. We suppose he took the ship, for that was the shortest way: along the west coast of the Gulf of Corinth, then diagonally across to the Port of Itea. Yes, and then it was only a few miles more uphill, through a pine forest, and soon he was standing outside the temples where Apollo lived, who, however, delivered the prophecy via a priestess, Pythia: a remnant from the time when, as Aeschylus reported, the oracle belonged to Gaia and her daughters Themis and Phoebe. (Jocasta's radical rejection of the oracle probably has to do with this changeover of power; she foams at the mouth whenever Delphi is mentioned, for she too is probably a relic from times when women—in her case queens—had a more autonomous position in Greek societies than in the classical Athens of Sophocles, in which the men very much had the say, Pericles, first and foremost, and the male gods, Apollo, first and foremost. How exactly, though, societies in those distant times were structured, we should very much like to know. The sources are so greatly at the mercy of our interpretations that there is space in them for the view that everything had always been as bleak as in classical Athens and nowadays—at most, a different kind of bleak—as well as for strong desires for a golden age of harmony, presided over by women. We don't know. Only men, in any case, stood on Sophocles' stage. And in the audience, too, only the men had any status, even if the occasional woman was allowed to watch. Independent, thinking women — Jocasta being one of them — weren't viewed kindly, at least by the men. Perhaps that's why, in the play competition at which *Oedipus the King* was premiered, Sophocles took only second place. Euripides, in any case, whose Medea was a frighteningly powerful female, had to flee to the altar during the premiere because pandemonium had broken out and the incensed spectators would have beaten him to death, otherwise. This was a year or two before *Oedipus* and on the same stage. So Sophocles had been warned.)

But let's move on. Oedipus reported to the serving priestess of the oracle, said what his question was — 'Who are my father and my mother?' — and was immediately given an appointment, as if she'd been waiting for him. 'You will recognize your father,' Pythia said, 'by slaying him, and your mother by having slept with her.'

Oedipus staggered outside. Never again, he realized right away, never again could he even be in the proximity of his dear parents. He mustn't return to Corinth! Killing Polybius! Sleeping with Merope! What a terrible notion!

And so he didn't return to the ship. Nor did he choose, however, when he came to the fork in the road, the path that would very definitely have led him away from danger, to the north. Instead, he envisaged a third path, one that would have brought him — a reference to his ambivalence, disguised as geography — via Thebes and Eleusis, by the overland route, to Corinth. He didn't get that far, however, as we know. Even before the parting of the roads, he was shooed to the side by a herald, walking ahead of a carriage in which only a king could be sitting. A herald and four bodyguards—only kings had these back then. But Oedipus was also from a royal dynasty and so didn't let himself be shooed into the ditch but tore strips off the herald, as only the sons of kings can. The whole entourage stopped and an old man sitting in the carriage—forty-five, he was, if he was a day—leant out the window and tried to clobber the insubordinate blackguard down on the road with his stick. Oedipus struck him dead. He also killed the herald and the bodyguards—apart from one, who took to his heels and instantly disappeared behind the gorse so quickly that Oedipus immediately forgot all about him. He didn't worry at all about what had happened—he was still too preoccupied with the message he'd received in Delphi— and continued energetically on his way, towards Thebes.

He didn't get as far, however, as *into* the town. For before it, up on a rock, lay the terrible Sphinx, not at all calmly, on her four paws, as if she were made of stone—no, in a flash, she could take on every thinkable and also every unthinkable shape and suddenly appear above you, before you, behind you. Her jaws were spitting fire, her teeth glowing. Young men, hundreds of them, were queuing in front of her. Hard to say what ideology, that had long since become their nature, had driven them to it. But, in

Sophocles' day, a barely comprehensible addiction to death in the Greek ruling class was part of everyday life. In Pericles' famous funeral oration for the men of Athens who had fallen in the war —held two or three years before *Oedipus the King*, and still remembered —the main motif is, likewise, the personal glorious deed of any man, and its heroic consummation in death. 'For heroes have the whole earth for their tomb.' — Not one young man in the queue, in any case, flinched away from the sacrifice. A scream ending suddenly, the crunching of bones, and the next one was already beneath the jaws that asked the question. Didn't know the answer, was eaten up. Oedipus joined the queue too and when, soon, he was at the front —the ground round the Sphinx, a bloody swamp meanwhile —he, too, saw the flaming eyes above him, the jaws wide open, the teeth like knives, he could smell the stink of sulphur, and heard the question the Sphinx howled, and answered, 'Man, of course.'

The Sphinx shrieked —so terribly that within a radius of ten miles birds fell dead from the sky —and threw herself from her rock. And fell far below, was smashed to pieces, a heap of scales, smelling of Hades and blood. Oedipus was carried into town by the jubilant people of Thebes —by women, mainly, for the strongest men had all been slashed to ribbons. He found a queen, Jocasta, who had just learnt, barely a few hours ago, that Laius, her husband, was dead. Serious, trembling, she congratulated the young male saviour and told him about the terrible thing that had happened to her. Her husband murdered, at a crossroads just below

Delphi! Only two days ago! As a reward for his incredible daring, she offered Oedipus the vacant throne and herself. (A queen like that must have seemed very unsettling in classical Athens.) Oedipus accepted immediately—he had, after all, been groomed to be king one day. He hadn't expected anything less. He was even—he just didn't know—the legitimate successor to Laius. Wine, songs of celebration, and again and again he had to describe what the jaws above him had been like. Such that, at about midnight, it also seemed quite natural to him that he'd inherited not merely a crown, but also a queen, and as if it were the most natural thing in the world, he slept with her in the same way that she saw a night of passion with this hero, who, if she counted the years between them, could have been her son, as something splendid and quite natural. Peaceful years again followed—again, eighteen of them. Happiness. Health. Good harvests. Jocasta and Oedipus had four splendid children, two girls, Ismene and Antigone, and two boys, Eteocles and Polynices. But then—Oedipus was now thirty-six, Jocasta just turned fifty—disaster returned to the town. Not a Sphinx, but the plague. The town burnt. The streets were full of people with no strength to crawl anywhere. The women had no more children. Corpses, wherever you looked.

And only now does the play begin, as we see it on the stage. Sophocles *shows* us only the final two to three hours of the whole drama: minute by minute, in real time. We're always in the same place, together with the residents of Thebes, who—while their salvation is being negotiated—

die by the dozen before our very eyes. (Athens had just had a plague epidemic; some sources say it was smallpox; each and every spectator, in any case, was someone who had just had another lucky escape and knew someone—a wife, a father, a child—who had died.)

The most senior members of the council call up to the palace windows: Oedipus, come out, you freed Thebes from a curse once before; who, if not you, can help us now? Oedipus, Oedipus.—Of course, he steps outside the palace gate. He has long since taken action and sent Creon, his wife's brother, to Delphi for help and advice. Yes, Creon's just come back with the message: Thebes will recover if Laius' murderer is caught and paid back. A message from Apollo that everyone—everyone but Jocasta—takes seriously, if only for the reason that the plague has been part of Apollo's repertoire since the year dot. He'd once directed it at the Greeks besieging Troy.—After some hours that pass breathlessly quickly, in which the only action is the steadily accentuating interplay between insight and resistance to insight, Oedipus is, in everyone else's eyes and also his own, the guilty party, dead, not physically dead, not yet, but dead in every other sense. Jocasta hangs herself. Oedipus gouges his eyes out with the long pins of her golden brooches and heads off, blind, bleeding, for the mountains where he was abandoned as a child, in order that he might die there, and the circle be completed.

The sand is racing so relentlessly from the upper part of the hourglass that is Oedipus' life into the lower part, you'd think it was aided by a sandblaster. The whole construct of Oedipus' life suddenly comes crashing down. It is as if he were plummeting into the empty universe and, free-falling, he tries to cling to everything that is falling with him.

For what must not be, cannot be: to this hope cling not only Oedipus, but all the others, the choir, Jocasta and even Creon. '"I have done that," says my memory,' as Nietzsche said, not of Oedipus. '"I cannot have done that," says my pride [. . .]. Eventually memory yields.'[31] And so the play has already ended several times, given that the solution that will save the town and destroy Oedipus has already been found, and yet it continues—the first time, rather bewilderingly, in the very first minutes, after only three hundred and fifty lines, when Tiresias looks the murderer who is hunting a murderer in the face, and says, 'You killed Laius.' It's too soon for everyone, and as if he hadn't said anything. The truth isn't the truth until it has been spoken. But it's also not the truth if the wrong person speaks it at the wrong time.

Sophocles' play, two thousand, four hundred and thirty years old, surprises us with a dramatic composition and virtuosic dialogues that seem very modern to us. Close to us. Right at the beginning of the history of theatre—together with the works of Aeschylus and Euripides—it achieved a high point in dramatic writing that was only reached again about two millennia later by Shakespeare who, with *Hamlet*, researched murder in a manner coloured by *Oedipus*, a play he later followed with *King Lear*, just as Sophocles, as an old man, followed his younger self's *Oedipus the King* with *Oedipus at Colonus*. As if both Sophocles and Shakespeare, as old men, had to think through to the end the thought behind their early plays. And their thoughts are similar. Lear, Shakespeare's old king, seems like a now older Hamlet to me, had the latter ever had the chance to become an old king. Confused, mad, not knowing who loves him. Was all the effort he put into life worth it? Oedipus the old man has turned out similarly, a confused person, acting with out-of-touch-with-the-real-world hubris as he goes to his death. Sophocles and Shakespeare: isn't it amazing that between them, in a period equal to about three hundred lifetimes, there is *nothing*, not a single text that comes even remotely close to the same level of poetic sensitivity and ability?

Yes, Shakespeare is the first to take up again what seems, already in Sophocles, so excitingly modern to us. Sophocles already knows much more about his characters than he tells us, and than they know themselves. His heroes don't say everything they know, and they don't always know what they are saying, because—as we would say today—their unconscious creeps into what they are saying. Everyone's concealing something from everyone else, and everyone—Oedipus, first and foremost—is concealing a lot also, especially, from themselves. Sophocles, however, knows what his heroes know and is also clear about what they are concealing from themselves. He knows the wrong tracks on which we end up due to what we nowadays call defence and repression. More than once, his heroes' words mean the opposite of the surface meaning. Sophocles knows what irony is.

It has often been said that *Oedipus the King* is a bit like a trial; a trial, however, in which the investigator, the culprit, the prosecutor and the judge are all one and the same person. A trial, nonetheless. And the verdict reached at the end — Oedipus is blinded and banished from the country — is indeed in keeping with the norms of jurisdiction in Athens at the time. — We are spectators at a trial based on circumstantial evidence. The accused denies committing the crime; yes, it's not even clear who the accused is. Everything revolves round the question: who knows what, and since when. Indeed, the whole excitement of the play has its roots in the fact that *everyone* senses or knows something, as does also, very soon, the spectator. In no one's case is the answer easy, not in Jocasta's, not in Creon's, not in the most senior council members' and certainly not in Oedipus'. Although, precisely in his case, we do have to wonder a lot. He had to have — he simply *must* have sensed something, known, not from the very beginning, but almost immediately. For he did, after all — not even two hours after the oracle prophesied that he'd kill his father — kill a man his father's age. A king, into the bargain. That cannot have escaped him, either. But no, nothing doing, Oedipus thinks absolutely nothing of it and goes to Thebes and is lying a few hours later in bed with the queen who is his mother's age, *his* mother's age, and who, between kisses, reports that her husband, the king, was killed only two days ago near

Delphi. Nothing, not even now, dawns on Oedipus, or at least he doesn't let it show, and sleeps the next night too and many future nights with his wife, whom—were he able to put two and two together—he would *have to* recognize as his mother. This cannot, as I said, be put down to a lack of intelligence. Sophocles, for sure, explicitly calls him one of the smartest of all mortals in order to rule out this possible explanation. Oedipus' cluelessness is, indeed, so difficult to accept that there are interpretations of the play that try to see Oedipus from the very beginning as someone who *knows* what he is doing, who has lived the past eighteen years as a kind of double-crosser, and who now tries, with disaster looming, to save his neck. Alternatively, when he sees that wouldn't succeed seeks the most suitable way and the best moment to allow the truth to become public.

This interpretation has something very seductive. Except, there is one thing it doesn't reckon with, and that, indeed, is repression and defence and the fact that—isn't that so?—memory says it was like this, the heart, however, says—if I may offer a variation on Nietzsche's words—that it *could not* have been.

Jocasta comes off best. Although, she too notices, immediately, the physical resemblance of her new husband to Laius; in bed with her lover, she also sees the latter's mutilated feet; and the fact that the only witness to the murder at first spoke about a single man and then, upon setting eyes on the new king, immediately withdrew his statement and began claiming that a whole band of robbers were the culprits, should also make her think. The witness also wanted to be permitted to leave town, right now, sooner than right away—a wish Jocasta generously granted—whereas, until then, he had been such a loyal servant to the royal house that he was even selected to take the unwanted child into the mountains. Be that as it may. Oedipus had not told her—unlike the other way round— about everything that had happened to him in the last few days. *She* was able to forget in the eighteen happy years how—curiously—immediately after Laius' death his successor had turned up.

And Creon? Creon, generally, comes off badly. He's the villain of the piece, usually. A power-hungry, slippery-as-an-eel politician who wants to become king himself and, after Oedipus' departure, indeed does. I think, nonetheless, that people do him a little injustice. For he, too—for as long as it suits the polis and the royal family for him to keep his mouth shut—is loyal, to the max. Now, however, considering the dying town and the second oracle, the max has been reached. Now, he can no longer support Oedipus, and it doesn't matter how many skeletons he has in his cupboard. Skeletons in the sovereign's cupboards leave someone like Creon cold as long as no one but him sees them. I think he knew about these skeletons from the beginning, right from the moment Oedipus wondrously turned up in the town. For, back then, he led the investigation into Laius' murder and was aware of all the contradictions. He placed all of this on file and closed the files at the moment Oedipus—to whom some pieces of circumstantial evidence pointed—was installed as king. He chose not to discuss with the only witness of the murder the inconsistencies in his statement and let him leave town without objection. Now he sees Oedipus wriggling and turning, and can imagine better than us why he is acting that way. 'If you want my report in the presence of these people, I am ready now, or we might go inside,'[32] he says at the beginning of the play, and later, when Oedipus, in ever tightening spirals, approaches the core of the insight: 'Natures like yours are hardest on themselves.'[33] Is that the way a pure-blooded schemer would speak? And right then he has to listen to the suggestion that he is planning a putsch in order to be king instead of Oedipus! Might he not think—the possibility occurs to us, at least—that the king wants him out of the way before he ends up being the key witness in a case that Oedipus wishes to avoid at all costs? You get the death penalty for high treason!—At the same time, Oedipus—not Creon—has long since set the real key witness in motion, that is, the surviving bodyguard. Throughout the whole play, *offstage*, he's getting closer and closer, and at the end, bang on time, he reaches the stage, breathless, and Oedipus is convicted. *High noon*, Greek-style.

But the story's far from over. With the moment when Oedipus—once and for all—realizes the truth and understands that he can't dodge it again, the story reaches its climax. 'Oi, oi, oi, now it's all come out!' Looking back from the real ending—years later in Colonus—we can risk stating that Oedipus, in his whole life, is clear-sighted only for these few minutes, and with justified humility and appropriate horror realizes what his situation is. But then, already in the first play, he begins again to become the old Oedipus, to outdo the old Oedipus, really blind now. Oedipus is simply *not* a seer, or is so only for these few minutes, however seduced we might be by the suggestion that he *sees* the moment he goes blind. No, just as a pain really hurts, blindness indeed makes you blind. Already as he staggers from the palace, covered in blood, he draws himself proudly up again—if, in life, you do not triumph, then at least be the greatest as you go down—like a sea captain whose ship has gone under and who now, swimming with whatever strength he has left, holds the mast up in the air. The play, by the way, doesn't only have losers, as in Oedipus and Jocasta, but it also has winners, the people of Thebes. While in the palace—unseen by us—Jocasta hangs herself and Oedipus blinds himself, the most senior council members and Creon are breathing again and patting one another's backs before our very eyes. The situation has been saved. The oracle has been fulfilled and the town is indeed already beginning to recover. The houses are no longer burning, those who—a moment ago—were dying, struggle to their feet, the first flowers begin to spring. If you *do not* look at things with Oedipus' eyes—a false picture, it's true— everything has turned out well again. Everyone's been saved, everyone but Oedipus and the unfortunate Jocasta, of course.—If, however, we read the play as a first self-analysis of human history — and we do tend in that direction — then this has failed spectacularly. Interpretation correct; the patient, blind.

But not dead yet. Twenty years later — Sophocles is ninety by now and will die soon — Oedipus is still alive, and let's assume for the sake of simplicity, also twenty years older. He's old, anyway. Antigone has become his eyes and, when necessary, his voice of reason, in line with reality. Sophocles hasn't kept the promise he made at the end of the first play. Oedipus hasn't gone into the mountains, he hasn't died at the spot where once everything began.

Why not? Why a second play at all? Because a story — if a dramatist is telling it — can only end tragically, and the tragic is always death. The finality of death cannot be outdone and all dramatists — Aeschylus, Shakespeare, Racine, Kleist — observe this rule. Only, this time — this *one* time — Sophocles had pulled off a tragic invention that couldn't be stepped up by having the hero die. The death of the hero *after* his realization, immediately after it, would have lessened the dismay at this insight and not increased it. And so the death was banished offstage and kept for later. And Sophocles, as an old man, then had the unexpected opportunity to re-interpret his story of an interpretation, and to have it end, now, finally, with the genuine ending of all tragedies, the death of the hero. He invents, shortly before his own death, a death apotheosis. We may assume that, with it, he was also alluding to himself a little.

In the story, as it is now told, Oedipus has remained in Thebes, on sufferance, wandering, lonely, through the alleys. Only now, so many years later, has he been sent fleeing, for a very Oedipal reason, tellingly. Polynices and Eteocles, his two now grown sons, are fighting over the crown that once was their father's and that now, provisionally so to speak, is waiting on Creon's head, who is—if we accept the rules of our time-reckoning game— sixty-eight meanwhile. Ancient, by the standards of the time. (Sophocles, who really existed, broke the mould with his ninety.)—Oedipus interrupts this quarrel to the death, and on the spur of the moment, the rival pretenders to the throne abandon their father somewhere outside the town, just as his own father had once done to him. But barely have they given their blind father the boot when a new oracle gets in their way, the fourth of the prophecies from Delphi that steer the story of Oedipus. It prophesies that Oedipus' burial place will bring good fortune in war to the owner of the land in question. With the consequence that nothing short of horse-trading breaks out as people vie for Oedipus' corpse, and the object of desire, fresh as a daisy still, is the most lively participant. Oedipus has the goods on-hand, of course, and so sells himself to the person who makes the best offer. To Theseus, the mythical king of Athens who, had he been the real one in Athens then, would indeed have urgently needed help for the following year, in 404 BCE, he will go on to lose the war against

Sparta, badly. Oedipus swaps his lucky-charm body for a dignified and appropriate death place in the most sacred district of Greece, that is, in Colonus, the dwelling place of the Eumenides, which a mortal otherwise cannot enter without being punished. (Colonus lies, still today, at the foot of the Acropolis and within sight of it. German translations have suggested to us that it was an island as the play—until Peter Handke's new translation—was always called Oedipus *on* Colonus. It's not an island, Colonus. It's a quiet residential area in Athens.)—Polynices, Eteocles and Creon are left standing, and Oedipus—a frenzied megalomaniac, an example of the ironic humour that can be found also in Sophocles' late work, emphatically warning his companion of the danger of madness—dies the most splendid of all deaths. Of course, he dies offstage, just as all the decisive moments in both Sophocles' plays happen outside our field of vision; and, of course, the only witness of this passing away, this return to the gods, can only report falteringly that he saw absolutely nothing, dazzled as he was by the greatness of the event. It is clear, at least, that the god—it can only be Apollo—fetched Oedipus personally.

That's what happens to Oedipus, in the end. What happens to Antigone, his adorable daughter, is much worse. *Her* death—the next instalment in this never-ending story— is what has given Creon such a rotten reputation. Not his roles in the Oedipus plays. Creon, you see, has Antigone buried alive, in strictly legal terms, because she defies his order to leave her dead brother lying on the battlefield for the ravens to eat, and tries to bury him. Creon's real reason, however, is more likely that he has not forgotten in how many ways Antigone's father offended him and that his son—the Oedipal stops at nothing, not even before the house of the rational pragmatist Creon—loves Antigone, and Antigone, Creon's son.

Freud, famously, while standing on the Acropolis and looking over Athens, suffered a feeling of derealization, and interpreted the experience in terms of surpassing his father, who had wished all his life to stand at this place—the very heart of classical culture—just once, and had never managed to. Definitely a reason to feel confused for a few meaningful moments. But perhaps too, who knows, Freud's gaze, unbeknown to him, passed over Oedipus' grave. It must be there somewhere, in Colonus, in the front garden of one of these petit-bourgeois villas, or right there, where the bus stops.

And so I have reached the end of my series of lectures. I liked being here and thank you for listening to me with so much patience.

Goodbye.

Notes

I am grateful to Seagull Books for enhancing this volume with the following notes and a bibliography. The information contained herein extends way beyond the sources I would have identified during my usual translation process. My thanks also to Urs Widmer who answered crucial questions and helped us identify important sources. — Trans.

1 Ilse Aichinger, *Herod's Children* (Cornelia Schaeffer trans.) (New York: Atheneum, 1963), p. 79. I have endeavoured to cite existing English translations of works wherever possible. Where translations do not exist, I have translated directly from the German. [Trans.]

2 A reference to mid-twelfth-century German poet Der von Kürenberg, who is best known for his poem 'Falconlied' (Falcon Song).

3 A reference to the second Merseburg Incantation, one of the two magic spells in Old High German, supposed to date from before the ninth century.

4 Walter Muschg, *Tragische Literaturgeschichte* (Zurich: Diogenes Verlag, 2006), p. 445.

5 Émile Cioran, *The Trouble with Being Born* (Richard Howard trans.) (New York: Viking, 1976), p. 78.

6 'Reservoir of rage' (*Zornreservoir*) is a key concept in Peter Sloterdijk's *Zorn und Zeit: Politisch-psychologischer Versuch* (Frankfurt: Suhrkamp Verlag, 2006).

7   Joseph Conrad to R. B. Cunninghame Graham, 8 February, 1899, in *The Collected Letters of Joseph Conrad*, VOL. 2, 1898–1902 (Frederick R. Karl and Laurence Davies eds) (Cambridge: Cambridge University Press, 1986), p. 160.

8   Samuel Beckett, *Waiting for Godot* (New York: Grove Press, 2011), p. 103.

9   Johann Wolfgang von Goethe to Johann Peter Eckermann, 4 February, 1829, in Johann Wolfgang von Goethe and Johann Peter Eckermann, *Conversations with Goethe in the Last Years of His Life* (Margaret Fuller trans.) (Hilliard, Gray, and company, 1839), p. 270.

10 Robert Walser, *Jakob von Gunten* (Christopher Middleton trans.) (New York: New York Review of Books, 1999), p. 154.

11 Gottfried Keller, *Der grüne Heinrich* (first version) in *Sämtliche Werke in acht Bänden*, VOL. 3 (Peter Goldammer ed.) (Berlin: Aufbau Verlag, 1958–61), pp. 9–892; here, p. 884.

12 Samuel Beckett, *Worstward Ho* (London: John Calder, 1983), p. 7.

13 Keller, *Sämtliche Werke in drei Bänden*, VOL. 3 (Clemens Heselhaus ed.) (Munich: Carl Hanser Verlag, 1958), p. 895.

14 Ibid.

15 Gottfried Keller, 'Denn uns gehört die ganze, schöne Welt!' (in 'Ihr nennt uns Träumer') in *Sämtliche Werke in acht Bänden*, VOL. 1 (Peter Goldammer ed.)(Berlin: Aufbau Verlag, 1958–61), pp. 53–4; 'O mein Heimatland! O mein Vaterland!' from 'An mein Vaterland', p. 128; 'Hurra! Hussa! Die Hatz geht los!' from 'Jesuitenlied', pp. 129–30; 'Bum! Bum! Bim, bam, bum' from 'Apostatenmarsch', pp. 131–3; 'Holde trikolore Dirne' from 'Überall!', pp. 135–6;

'Hebt den Schild' from 'Überall!', pp. 135–6; 'O Maienlust, o Freiheitsbaum' from 'Der Freiheitsbaum', pp. 137–8.

16 Gottfried Keller, 'Winter Night' in *Selected Translations: 1968–1978* (William Stanley Merwin trans.) (New York: Atheneum, 1979), p. 148.

17 Walter Benjamin, 'Gottfried Keller' in *Selected Writings*: VOL. 2, PART 1, 1927–1930 (Michael William Jennings, Howard Eiland and Gary Smith eds) (Rodney Livingstone trans.) (Cambridge, MA: Harvard University Press, 2005), pp. 51–61; here, p. 56.

18 Gottfried Keller, 'Frau Regel Amrain und ihr Jüngster' in *Die Leute von Seldwyla* (Brunswick: Friedrich Vieweg and Son, 1856), pp. 113–208; here p. 124.

19 Ibid., p. 125.

20 Ibid., p. 208.

21 Keller, *Der grüne Heinrich*, p. 887.

22 Quoted in John Firman Coar (ed.), *Studies in German Literature in the Nineteenth Century* (London: Macmillan, 1903).

23 Keller, *Der grüne Heinrich*, p. 892.

24 Sigmund Freud, *A General Introduction to Psychoanalysis* (G. Stanley Hall trans.) (New York: Horace Liveright, 1920), p. 327.

25 Quoted in Richard P. Sugg (ed.), *Jungian Literary Criticism* (Evanston, Il: Northwestern University Press, 1992), p. 67.

26 Johann Wolfgang von Goethe, *Truth and Poetry: From My Own Life* (John Oxenbridge trans.) (London: Henry G. Bohn, 1848), p. 1. Available at: http://archive.org/stream-/autobiographyofg00goetuoft#page/n13/mode/2up

27 Quoted in Maxime Du Camp, *Souvenirs littéraires: Flaubert, Fromentin, Gautier, Musset, Nerval, Sand* (Brussels: Editions Complexe, 2002), p. 126.

28 Goethe, *Truth and Poetry*, p. 47.

29 Jean Paul, *Sämmtliche Werke*, VOL. 32 (Berlin: Georg Reimar Verlag, 1842), p. 80.

30 Urs Widmer, 'König Ödipus'. *Akzente* 52 (2005): 521–33.

31 Friedrich Nietzsche, *Beyond Good and Evil: Prelude to a Philosophy of the Future* (Walter Kauffmann trans.) (New York: Vintage, 1989), p. 80.

32 Sophocles, *The Three Theban Plays* (Robert Fagles trans., Bernard Knox introd and annot.) (London and New York: Penguin Books, 1984), p. 163.

33 Ibid., p. 198.

AICHINGER, Ilse. *Herod's Children* (Cornelia Schaeffer trans.). New York: Atheneum, 1963.

BECKETT, Samuel. *Krapp's Last Tape* in *Krapp's Last Tape and Other Dramatic Pieces*. New York: Grove Press, 1994, pp. 7–28.

———. *Waiting for Godot*. New York: Grove Press, 2011.

———. *Worstward Ho*. London: John Calder, 1983.

BENJAMIN, Walter. 'Gottfried Keller' in *Selected Writings*, VOL. 2, PART 1, 1927–1930 (Michael William Jennings, Howard Eiland and Gary Smith eds, Rodney Livingstone trans.). Cambridge, MA: Harvard University Press, 2005, pp. 51–61.

CERVANTES, Miguel de. *Don Quixote* (John Rutherford trans.). London and New York: Penguin Books, 2003.

CHEKHOV, Anton. *Uncle Vanya* (Christopher Hampton trans.). London: Faber and Faber, 2012.

CIORAN, Émile. *The Trouble with Being Born* (Richard Howard trans.). New York: Viking, 1976.

COAR, John Firman (ed.). *Studies in German Literature in the Nineteenth Century*. London: Macmillan, 1903.

CONRAD, Joseph. *The Collected Letters of Joseph Conrad*, VOL. 2, 1898–1902 (Frederick R. Karl and Laurence Davies eds). Cambridge: Cambridge University Press, 1986.

DICKENS, Charles. *David Copperfield*. London and New York: Penguin Classics, 1997.

DU CAMP, Maxime. *Souvenirs littéraires: Flaubert, Fromentin, Gautier, Musset, Nerval, Sand*. Brussels: Editions Complexe, 2002.

FREUD, Sigmund. *A General Introduction to Psychoanalysis* (G. Stanley Hall trans.). New York: Horace Liveright, 1920.

GOETHE, Johann Wolfgang von. *Elective Affinities* (David Constantine trans.). Oxford and New York: Oxford University Press, 2008.

——. *Faust: A Tragedy* (Cyrus Hamlin ed., Walter Arndt trans.). London and New York: W. W. Norton, 2001.

——. *Truth and Poetry: From My Own Life* (John Oxenbridge trans.). London: Henry G. Bohn, 1848. Available at http://archive.org-/stream/autobiographyofg00goetuoft#page/n13/mode/2up

——. 'Welcome and Farewell' (Christopher Middleton trans.) in Christopher Middleton (ed.), *Johann Wolfgang von Goethe: Selected Poems*, VOL. 1. Boston: Suhrkamp/Insel, 1983.

—— and Johann Peter Eckermann. *Conversations with Goethe in the Last Years of His Life* (Margaret Fuller trans.). Boston: Hilliard, Gray, and Company, 1839. Available at http://books. google.-co.in/books?id=Yi0HAAAAQAAJ&printsec=frontcover&source =gbs_ge_summary_r&cad=0#v=onepage&q&f=false

GOTTHELF, Jeremias. *The Black Spider* (Jolyon Timothy Hughes trans.). Lanham, MD: University Press of America, 2010.

GRASS, Günter. *The Tin Drum* (Ralph Manheim trans.). New York: Pantheon, 1961.

HALLER, Albrecht von. 'The Alps' in *The Poems of Baron Haller* (J. Howorth trans.). London: J. Bell, 1794.

JOYCE, James. *Finnegans Wake*. Hertfordshire: Wordsworth Classics, 2012.

——. *Ulysses*. London: Penguin Classics, 2000.

KELLER, Gottfried. *The Banner of the Upright Seven* (Bayard Quincy Morgan trans.). Whitefish, MT: Kessinger Publishing, 2004.

——. *Der grüne Heinrich* (first version) in *Sämtliche Werke in acht Bänden*, VOL. 3 (Peter Goldammer ed.). Berlin: Aufbau Verlag, 1958–61, pp. 9–892.

——. 'Frau Regel Amrain und ihr Jüngster' in *Die Leute von Seldwyla*. Brunswick: Friedrich Vieweg and Son, 1856, pp. 113–208.

——. *Martin Salander* (Kenneth Halwas trans.). London: John Calder, 1964.

——. *The People of Seldwyla* in *The People of Seldwyla and Seven Legends* (M. D. Hottinger trans.). London and Toronto: J. M. Dent and Sons, 1929.

——. *Sämtliche Werke in acht Bänden*, VOL. 1 (Peter Goldammer ed.). Berlin: Aufbau Verlag, 1958–61.

——. *Sämtliche Werke in drei Bänden*, VOL. 3 (Clemens Heselhaus ed.). Munich: Carl Hanser Verlag, 1958.

——. 'Winter Night' in William Stanley Merwin (trans.), *Selected Translations: 1968–1978*. New York: Atheneum, 1979.

MANN, Thomas. *Buddenbrooks: Decline of a Family* (John E. Wood trans.). New York: Everyman's Library, 1994.

——. *The Magic Mountain* (John E. Woods trans., A. S. Byatt introd). New York: Everyman's Library, 2005.

——. *A Man and His Dog* (Herman George Scheffauer trans.). New York: Alfred A. Knopf, 1930.

MELVILLE, Herman. *Moby Dick* (Tony Tanner ed.). Oxford and New York: Oxford University Press, 2008.

MILLER, Henry. *Big Sur and the Oranges of Hieronymus Bosch*. New York: New Directions, 1957.

——. *The Colossus of Maroussi*. New York: New Directions, 2010.

——. *Tropic of Cancer*. New York: Grove Press, 1961.

MUSCHG, Walter. *Tragische Literaturgeschichte*. Zurich: Diogenes Verlag, 2006.

MUSIL, Robert. *The Man without Qualities*, VOLS 1 and 2 (Sophie Wilkins and Bernard Pike trans). New York: Vintage, 1996.

NIETZSCHE, Friedrich. *Beyond Good and Evil: Prelude to a Philosophy of the Future* (Walter Kauffmann trans.). New York: Vintage, 1989.

NONNENMANN, Klaus. *Teddy Flesh oder Die Belagerung von Sagunt*. Olten, Freiburg: Walter Verlag, 1964.

PLATEN, August von. *Der romantische Oedipus*. Tübingen: J. G. Cottaische Buchhandlung, 1829.

PROUST, Marcel. *In Search of Lost Time* (C. K. Scott Moncrieff, Terence Kilmartin and Andreas Mayor trans). New York: Modern Library, 2003.

SHAKESPEARE, William. *Hamlet* (Cyrus Hoy ed.). London and New York: W. W. Norton, 1992.

———. *Macbeth* (Robert S. Miola ed.). London and New York: W. W. Norton, 2004.

———. *Titus Andronicus* (Alan Hughes ed.). Cambridge: Cambridge University Press, 2006.

SLOTERDIJK, Peter. *Zorn und Zeit: Politisch-psychologischer Versuch*. Frankfurt: Suhrkamp Verlag, 2006.

SOPHOCLES. *The Three Theban Plays* (Robert Fagles trans., Bernard Knox introd and annot.). London and New York: Penguin Books, 1984.

STIFTER, Adalbert. *Witiko*. Leipzeig: C. F. Amelang, 1865–67.

SUGG, Richard P. (ed.). *Jungian Literary Criticism*. Evanston, IL: Northwestern University Press, 1992.

TOLSTOY, Leo. *War and Peace* (Constance Garnett trans., A. N. Wilson introd). New York: Modern Library, 2004.

WALSER, Robert. *The Assistant* (Susan Bernofsky trans.). New York: New Directions, 2007.

———. 'Eine Weihnachtsgeschichte' in *Sämtliche Werke in Einzelausgaben*, VOL. 16 (Jochen Greven ed.). Frankfurt: Suhrkamp Verlag, 1985, pp. 61–6.

———. *Jakob von Gunten* (Christopher Middleton trans.). New York: New York Review of Books, 1999.

———. *The Robber* (Susan Bernofsky trans.). Winnipeg: Bison Books, 2000.

———. *The Walk* (Susan Bernofsky and Christopher Middleton trans). New York: New Directions, 2012.

WIDMER, Urs. 'König Ödipus'. *Akzente* 52 (2005): 521–33.